503 WORLD'S WORST DIRTY JOKES

❊503❊
WORLD'S
WORST
DIRTY
JOKES

Previously Titled

ANECDOTA AMERICANA
SERIES TWO

With New Illustrations by

JAMES L. KRUYSMAN

& a New Foreword

BELL PUBLISHING COMPANY
NEW YORK

This book was originally published in 1934,
in a slightly different form, as *Anecdota
Americana*—Series Two.

Publisher's Note: The names used in this
book are purely fictitious and any resemblance
to persons living or dead is entirely coincidental.

This 1982 edition is published by Bell Publishing Company.

h   g   f   e   d   c   b

Manufactured in the United States of America

Library of Congress Cataloging in Publication Data

503 world's worst dirty jokes.

   Originally published: 1934.
    1. Sex—Anecdotes, facetiae, satire, etc.
I. Anecdota Americana.   II. Title.
III. Title: Five hundred three.
PN6231.S54H29   1982   818′.5402′08   82-1230
ISBN: 0-517-371642   AACR2

FOREWORD

From the midst of the uninhibited eighties, it is difficult to imagine the climate of suppression and repression that existed in this country in the late twenties and early thirties. Where the media were concerned, the racey and ribald were definitely off limits.

But that didn't stop people from enjoying dirty jokes, telling them and collecting them. And, in 1929, a small group of determined men, which included writers and artists (some of them notable), gathered together a compendium of 500 erotic tales and printed it privately under the title *Anecdota Americana*. The limited edition was a whopping success and quickly became a collector's item. (It has recently been reprinted by Bell Publishing Company as *The Classic Book of Dirty Jokes*.) Six years later they followed it with *Anecdota Americana – Series Two*, published in the same manner. On the title page, they described this as "An Anthology of Tales in the Vernacular – Edited without Expurgation," which puts the case mildly. Encouraged by the success of the original *Anecdota Americana* and the gradually liberalizing temper of 1935, they produced an even more outrageous volume. Whereas the first collection concentrated on the lewd and lascivious, this book went further—it was rude, crude and downright offensive to many groups and sensibilities. In fact, one could say that every other joke is at someone's expense. No group has been spared: the Irish, Scotch, Jews, Chinese, Roumanians, English, Italians, Swedes, French, Germans,

Russians, Southerners, homosexuals, lesbians, and more—all have been attacked. And in a vein contemporary with the times, there are numerous references to Nazis.

So, here, not for the faint-hearted, fastidious, or even the discriminating, are 503 of the world's worst dirty jokes!

PREFACE

More than six years have passed since the first volume of these anecdotes appeared. Spurred on by the depression, prohibitions are being repealed, taboos and censorships lifted.

The anecdotes herewith presented are part and parcel of the current folk-lore of America. They are an authentic source of American proletarian art. No excuse is needed or offered in passing them on to the reading public.

The stories are printed as they are told by word-of-mouth. If the gentle reader still burdened with Victorian hangovers finds some of them difficult to stomach, it might be well for him to strengthen his digestion. We are proud to give him the opportunity of doing so.

J. M. H.

These tall tales, as a token of everlasting friendship, to my college chum Jim.

J. M. H.

·1·

Do you know the difference between a gigolo, a doctor, a rabbi, and a chorus girl? ¶ A gigolo is a penis vendor, a doctor is a penis mender, a rabbi is a penis ender, and a chorus girl is a penis bender.

·2·

A husband and wife decided that they would make this a sensible Christmas. They talked over what they each wanted and decided to give the desired objects as presents. The wife wished a diamond bracelet and the husband a platinum wrist-watch. ¶ On Christmas morning the wife looked under the tree only to find a large package for herself, containing a silk dress. She was furious and threw the dress on the floor wiping her feet on it. ¶ Then the husband came in, and he also found a large package awaiting him. He opened it to find a pair of pants, which he threw upon the tree in a fit of anger. ¶ That afternoon as they were having Christmas dinner, the wife found in front of her place at the table, a small box containing the desired bracelet. The husband likewise found a package at his place containing the wrist-watch. They were very happy, so he picked up her dress and she pulled down his pants and they had a Merry Christmas.

·3·

A priest was walking up Eighth Avenue in the red-light district of New York City when a young woman standing in a doorway shouted out to him, "Head! Ten Dollars!" Not knowing what the woman meant by "head," the priest continued walking up the avenue, but again, a young woman standing in a doorway shouted out to him, "Head! Ten Dollars!" Confused, the priest paused and was about to ask the woman what she meant; but upon seeing the manner in which she was dressed, he decided that she was one that he could not associate himself with. He continued walking up the avenue only to hear more shouts of "Head! Ten Dollars!" When he arrived at his church, he spotted the Mother Superior and quickly asked her, "Mother Superior, what's 'head'?" She replied, " 'Head'? Ten dollars, same as on Eighth Avenue!"

·4·

Moe and George were sitting in a steambath. Moe was really, really fat, and George remarked, "I can't believe how fat you've gotten." Moe replied, "I'm so fat, I can't even see my putz anymore." So George asked, "Why don't you diet?" "Dye it! Dye it!" yelled Moe, "Why, what color is it now?"

·5·

Young Man: Do you know the difference between a chef salad and a blow job?
Young Woman: No.
Young Man: Good, let's have lunch tomorrow.

·6·

What is the difference between a pious woman and a woman taking a bath?
A pious woman has hope in her soul and . . .

·7·

Bunny was unfortunate enough to be arrested for sucking a cock. At the trial, the judge, who was of French descent, asked that the evidence of the crime be produced before the court. ¶ The arresting officer looked puzzled and asked, "How can I show evidence, your honor? He swallowed it."

·8·

In a jubilant mood, Bunny took the street car for home. A fellow sitting beside him, nudged him slyly and whispered. "Some beautiful pair of legs on that dame opposite, eh buddy?" ¶ "Yes," said Bunny, "but look at the beautiful ass on that motorman."

·9·

Saint Peter, according to an Affiliated Press dispatch from the Hereafter, was roused from a doze by the approach of a kindly but somewhat pompous gentleman. Peter, after ascertaining the name of the gentleman, asked what his occupation might have been on earth. ¶ "I am a psycho-analyst," was the reply. ¶ "What's that?" asked Peter. ¶ "A psycho-analyst," explained the newcomer, "helps maladjusted people to get adjusted, resolves complexes, restores mental health and emotional equilibrium, removes delusions of grandeur." ¶ Peter regarded him dubiously. "You say you remove delusions of grandeur?" ¶ "We endeavor to," said the analyst, somewhat more modestly. "Sometimes we succeed." ¶ "By all means come in, God thinks He's Hitler and wants to lick the hole of France."

·10·

A Philadelphia and a New York whore were talking shop and the Philadelphia girl asked, "How is business in New York these days?" ¶ "Business is pretty bad. Why a girl is lucky if she can get a dollar for a lay." ¶ "I should call that pretty good business. Why in Philadelphia we're sucking pricks for food."

·11·

A seafaring man, having acquired a buxom wife, quit his ship and decided to settle down. The only reminder of his boisterous days on the rolling main was a foul-mouthed parrot, to which he had become attached. ¶ As the months passed, however, his wife complained so often of the bird's swearing, that, in order to maintain peace in the family, he cut its throat and threw it into the toilet. ¶ A little while later, his wife, who was unwell, went to the bathroom to fulfill one of nature's calls. She had been in the cabinet only a few minutes when the sailor heard a piercing cry. ¶ Rushing into the W.C., he heard a voice issue from the depths of the china bowl: "If anybody can have a cut like that and still be alive, then I guess I can live too!"

·12·

For some time Mrs. Smith had been planning a picnic for her dear little children. The day before the event she was busy making elaborate preparations. ¶ "Mamma." cried little Willie from upstairs, "Jane has locked herself in the bath-room, and the boarder can't get in to take a shit." ¶ "Alright," said Mamma, "Jane can't go to the picnic." ¶ "Mamma" called Johnnie, "Edith pissed in the bread box and is floating paper boats in it." ¶ "For that Edith can't go to the picnic either." ¶ "Mamma" cried Eddie, "Willie has his finger up Edith's cunt and Johnnie just shit in the sandwich basket." ¶ "God damn it, there'll be no bloody picnic," said mamma.

·13·

The shortest bedtime story: "No."

·14·

A little girl was in the habit of buying chocolate candy babies every day at the local candy store. The clerk inquired of her one day why she always wished little boy candies. ¶ "Because," she answered. "I get more that way."

·15·

Sanitary napkin theme song: "I cover the waterfront."

·16·

A country boy came to the big city and noticing all the billiard parlors around town, decided they were drinking establishments. He came to a real saloon, and trying to look very sophisticated, entered and said to the bartender of the crowded establishment, "Give me a large billiard." ¶ The bartender winked at some of the other customers, took a glass, went into the back room and pissed in it. He handed it to the stranger, who blew the foam off the top, and drank the entire contents in one gulp. He then turned to the fellow standing next to him and said, "You know, if it wasn't for the fact that I've been drinking billiards for years, I would have sworn that was piss."

·17·

The very ritzy Mrs. Goldenwasser had a little daughter, Sylvia, who was in the habit of saying "I wish to pee-pee." when she wanted to go to the toilet. ¶ Mrs. G. considered this very unrefined and decided to break her daughter of the habit. She was planning a swanky bridge party next day for the ladies of the local chapter of the B'Nai Brith and was particularly anxious to impress the members. ¶ After diligent rehearsing, she finally taught Sylvia to wave her hand in front of her face when she wished to make pee-pee. ¶ At the party the next day all went well until the pastrami sandwiches and other delicacies were served. Just as Mrs. G. was urging the elegant Mrs. Fleishenheimer to partake of a lox sandwich on rye bread, little Sylvia ran into the room frantically waving her hand in front of her face. ¶ "All right dear, I understand," said Mrs. G. "You can run along." ¶ "But mamma," said Sylvia loudly, continuing to wave her hand. "Shit too!"

·18·

There was a terrible commotion in front of a Parisian Hotel. A man in one of the rooms had been screaming blue murder for an hour. A large crowd had gathered and finally the Gendarmerie arrived on the scene and rushed up to the man's room. They broke down the door and found him sitting on the edge of the bed, clutching his prick for dear life. ¶ "What is the matter," they asked. ¶ "I weel tell you the story from the beginning. Last night I go to the Opera. In the lobby ees a beautiful woman, such beauty as you have never seen before gentlemen, believe me. She flirt wiz me and we go to Zelli's. You know Zelli's, gentlemen, zee highest price night club in all of Paree. We drink champagne all night and I spend one, two, three thousand francs. Zen she ask weel I take her to the hotel George V. Gentlemen, you know the hotel George V, zee most expensive hotel in all of Paree. I pay a thousand francs for zee royal suite for zee night. Zen zees beautiful woman she take off all her clothes. ¶ "Mon Dieu, gentlemen, nevair have you seen such a body. Breasts like zee top of zee cafe Du Dome, gentlemen, and a cunt more magnificent than the Arc De Triomph. Zen she stretch out on ze bed and ask me to please come and fuck her. ¶ "And what do you think this little bastard do, gentlemen? Zis little bastard weel not get zee hard on. She play wit' heem and suck heem and stroke heem in the gentlest manner, but gentlemen he weel not get zee erection. ¶ "But now I get even on heem, gentlemen, now I get even on heem. He wishes to pee for zee last hour and I won't let heem."

·19·

Two cockneys were chatting on diverse subjects, when Alf turns to 'Arry and says, ¶ "'Ave you ever taysted 'orse-piss, 'Arry?" ¶ "Cahn't say that I 'ave, Alf," replied his friend. ¶ "Well," returned 'Arry consolingly, "You ayn't missed much!"

·20·

Rosenberg had made a lot of money and he thought, "Vat goot is haffing money if you can't show your frands you got it?" ¶ So he bought a magnificent home and furnished it without thinking of the expense. Everything in the house was the latest and best and every time he'd meet an old friend he'd take him up to see his wonderful home. ¶ One day he met his old friend Cohen, whom he knew when he was on the lower East side in the pushcart business, and whom he now took up to see his house. ¶ "Und dis, Cohen, is mine modern bath room," he was telling his friend. "Dis bath tub is made of the finest cut glass. Und dese shelves, they are all pure rose vood, mind you, pure rose vood." ¶ "Vat I vant to see," said Cohen. "Iss dis pre-heated toilet you got in your place. Vere iss it?" ¶ "Pre-heated toilet? Who told you I got a pre-heated toilet?" ¶ "I mat Ginsboig de odder day, and he told me you got a pre-heated toilet here." ¶ "Vy dat sonaffabitch Ginsboig, he's de vone vat shit in my fireless cooker."

·21·

"Marie, I've known you for a long time. Don't you think it's about time you let me put my tool into you?" "All right, Sam, you come out into the alley and we'll get together." They went out to the alley but when she saw the size of Sam's tool she moaned and said, "My, I could never take that tool in me, it's much too large." "Well, that ain't no reason for letting it drop in the mud!"

·22·

Definition of a vasectomy: Dry sack on the rocks.

·23·

Maizie was before a court of justice because her husband had died at the crucial moment when they were fucking one night. "Judge," said Maizie, "I couldn't help it. When I thought that man was coming, he sure was going."

·24·

A young priest was hearing the confession of a man who said his besetting sin was sucking cocks. It was the cleric's first encounter with this particular sexual activity, and he was at a loss for the proper penance to impose. After some cogitation he excused himself for a moment and sought another priest, to whom he related the confession he had just heard. ¶ "I don't know what to give him," he concluded. ¶ "Oh," said the older priest, "give him a dollar or so if you feel like it. Personally, I never give them more than 50 cents."

·25·

Two sparrows flying over Germany. Suddenly Hitler appears on the steps of the Reich. "Well," said one sparrow to the other. "What are you waiting for?"

·26·

Mrs. Murphy and Mrs. Kelly had had a terrible argument across the alley that separated their flats. Mrs. Murphy lost her temper and stuck her big fat bare ass out of the window at Mrs. Kelly. Not to be outdone, Mrs. Kelly did the same and both women remained in this position until finally Mr. Murphy came home from work. ¶ "What in hell do you call this Maggie? Shure and I'm coming from me days work hungry and tired and here you be with yer ass a sticking out of the window." ¶ "Yes, and here it is I'll stay until Mrs. Kelly takes her ass in first." ¶ "Well I think it's right you are, but let me stick my ass out while you're gettin' me supper, she won't know the difference." ¶ So Mr. Murphy took down his pants and stuck his ass out the window. ¶ Soon Mr. Kelly came home from work hungry and tired. He received the same answer from his wife, as had Murphy. ¶ "Well darlin'," said he, "I'm very hungry and tired, but you might as well stick it out now, for I'm shure she won't last long, her guts is already hanging down about eight inches from her ass-hole."

"In the lobby ees a beautiful woman."

·27·

After a strenuous meeting of Brown-shirts the night before, Adolph Hitler awoke in the morning with a terrible pain in his prick, and, on closer examination found a peculiar spot on the head. ¶ He consulted his private physician, who like himself had been a house-painter before he had come into the power of Germany. ¶ "Ah Adolph," said the physician, "What a beautiful instrument you have there, but I think the trouble with you is just a little bit of clap." ¶ This explanation did not satisfy Adolph, who called the doctor a dirty Jew and sent him away. ¶ He next consulted the finest specialist in all Germany, who had been a beer dispenser before Herr Hitler bestowed that title on him. ¶ "Ah Adolph," said he, "never before has your tool looked so magnificent, but I believe you have just a bit of a shanker on the head." ¶ Adolph sent him away in disgust, calling him a normal son-of-a-bitch and summoned the chef whose name was Cohen, and who had been a world famous venerial specialist before the Hitler regime. ¶ "Herr Hitler," said he, "I must admit that you have a very beautiful piece of meat and I should like very much to taste of it." ¶ Being granted this favor by the almighty Adolph, the chef said, "Herr Hitler, it tastes like there might be a bit of shit on the end of your prick." ¶ Herr Hitler sighed, and thinking of the important meeting of the night before said, "It's very possible, very possible."

·28·

A Pennsylvania coal miner was coaxing his wife, "Come on, Nell, how's about it for a lay tonight?" ¶ "Can't John," she answered, "Me cunt is in no condition for fucking tonight." ¶ "How about a piece of ass then?" said he, not being easily discouraged. ¶ "Be Jesus Christ, you men. First you muck up me fuck hole and now you wants to fuck up me muck hole."

·29·

He had been concealing the fact that he had a wooden leg from his bride to be, for a long time. "Honey," he would say to her, "The night that we are married I have a big surprise for you." ¶ Finally that eventful night came and still he had been unable to break the news to the bride. When they were about to go to bed he said, "Darling, let's put out the light before we undress." When the light was out she said, "Don't forget darling, you promised me a big surprise tonight." ¶ He had taken off the wooden leg and taking her hand put it on the stump. ¶ "Mmmm," she said, "that is a big surprise, but get the vaseline and I'll see if I can take it."

·30·

Suggested slogan for sanitary napkins: ¶ "Next to the best thing in the world."

·31·

A man made a wager with a bar-tender that he could guess the make and year and vintage of every drink in the house. If he guessed them all correctly, they were to be free of charge. But if he missed once, he was to pay for all he had consumed. ¶ He started off with a white liquid, tasted it, rolled it around his tongue for a moment and said, "That's Bordon's Gin, bottled in 1918." ¶ "That's right!" said the bar-tender. "Now try this." and he handed the man another drink. He repeated the process and said, "That's Smith Champagne, of the year 1921." ¶ He was right again and was then given a drink of brandy, which he guessed was Bartell's 1905. ¶ The bar-tender, beginning to be worried by the loss of profits he would have to make up out of his own pocket, called some of the boys at the bar together and they stepped into the back room for a minute, returning with a glass of yellow liquid. The man gulped it, rolled it around a bit, swallowed it and said, "Gentlemen, that's piss." ¶ "We know it's piss," said the bar-tender. "But whose is it?"

·32·

He had a plantation in South America where two hundred and fifty native women were employed. Things were going smoothly, until one day the women came to him *en masse* and demanded that he get a man for them. They didn't care where or what kind of a man, but they must have a man or they would all go on strike. ¶ He had tried all over South America to get a suitable man to do the job, but to no avail. Next he came to the United States and after searching all over the country, finally saw in Tennessee a man who could probably meet the requirements. ¶ Sammy, as the man was called, was a big six-foot-two good-looker, with perhaps the largest prick in the United States and the reputation of being able to fuck more times in a night than any other fellow in the South. ¶ "Sammy," he was asked, "How would you like to earn a hundred dollars?" ¶ "I sure would, man. What doin'?" ¶ "It's the sort of job I think you'll like. Take a trip with me to South America, fuck every woman on my plantation and I'll pay your fare back to Tennessee and give you one hundred dollars besides." ¶ "How many women you all got on that plantation o' yourn?" ¶ "Only two hundred and fifty, Sammy." ¶ "How long it take to get to that there South America?" ¶ "Oh, the trip should take about fifteen days." ¶ Sammy seemed to be figuring something out very seriously, and, after pondering for about ten minutes he asked. "How many times you all want me to fuck each woman?" ¶ "Three or four times each Sammy, three or four times each." ¶ "No sir, I cain't do it. I ain't gonna travel all that distance for half an hours work, nohow."

·33·

Girls who frequent picture palluces
Have no use for psycho-analysus;
They can't be annoyed
By fellows like Freud
But stick to their old fashioned phallices.

·34·

Miss Pauline Smith moved to a small town where the post office was in a general store owned by a dolt. ¶ Every day she would go in the store to inquire for a letter she was expecting. "Good morning, Miss Pauline," the proprietor would say, "Sorry dere ain't no mail for you today, Miss Pauline." ¶ This went on for about a week and one day she said, "Are you sure there's no mail for me? I'm expecting a very urgent letter. Would you look under the name of Smith and make sure?" ¶ "Oh, oh, oh, so Smith is your name. All this time I've been looking in de P hole and now I'll haff to start looking in de S hole."

·35·

Heard in a Greenwich Village restaurant . . . ¶ "I hear the authorities are going to collect all the women in the city, put them in the Holland Tunnel and seal the ends." ¶ "Goody, Goody," from one of the patrons. "Then all the men will have to use the ferries."

·36·

John came home from the coal mines looking very sad and dejected one evening. ¶ "What's the matter, John?" asked Nell. "You look as though your prick might have been cut off." ¶ "No Nell," said he. "But it's almost as bad as that, I've lost me job at the mines." ¶ "Oh, Johnnie, that's too bad. But come out on the front porch, I have something to show you." ¶ They went out on the front porch and she said, "You see those four houses, John, they all belong to us." ¶ John looked at her incredibly, and asked, "But how did you do it Nellie, how in hell did you get all those houses?" ¶ "Well, you see John, every time you threw a fuck into me, I put a penny in the bank and saved enough to buy the four houses." ¶ "Gee, honey," said he, "you're a wonderful wife." ¶ "Yes, but you're not a wonderful husband, for if you'd a been true to me we could a had the saloon on the corner to boot."

·37·

The Georgia Jennings, as they were known all through the south, sat around the roaring fire in the drawing room having their after dinner brandy and coffee. A grand old family with a grand old name in the grand old mansion which had been in the family for generations. They were justly proud of the prestige which they had maintained during these years, proud of the money they had accumulated in the family, and above all, proud of the name of Jennings, which any one of them would have defended with his life. Colonel Jennings, who was a typical example of the southern gentleman with fine white beard, a frock coat that his grandfather had worn during the Civil War and a gold chain across his waistcoat was addressing the gathering in a slow monotonous quiet voice, as is the habit of all southern gentlemen. "Rosa-Belle," said he to his daughter, "You are a much better fuck than your old mammy here." ¶ "That's what brother Stephen always told me, dad." answered Rosa-Belle. ¶ "But, dad," put in Stephen. "Rosa-Belle tells me that Uncle George sucks a cunt with much more gusto than you do, and I know for a fact that mother is a much better ass-hole sucker than Rosa-Belle." ¶ And they all drank a toast to the name of Jennings.

·38·

Two stately southern colonels alighted from a train at Birmingham. Their white beards blew in the wind as they accumulated their baggage and tipped the porter handsomely. ¶ Asked one of the other, "Well, Stephen, shall we check in at a hotel, or shall we go directly to the whore-house?"

·39·

There was the man who boasted he could fuck seventy times a night, once in bed and sixty-nine on the floor.

•40•

Stock-market tip: Allied Fruit stock is the best buy of the season. Insiders say it may go to 500. They've developed a banana that pulsates!

•41•

"Oh John," said Mary, "I don't mind you having your finger up my cunt, but your ring is hurting me." ¶ "Why I'm not wearing a ring Mary, that's my wristwatch."

•42•

Little Willie was jerking-off up in a tree, when a kindly old lady came along and advised him. "Little boy, you shouldn't do that. Don't you know that every time you come it might be a president, or a great baseball player, or an actor, or a great aviator?" ¶ Just then Little Willie came off, and as the come dripped from branch to branch and landed gracefully at the lady's feet, he said. "Holy Christ, lady, I guess you're right, there goes an acrobat."

•43•

Mike went to the doctor, who examined him and told him to return the following day with a specimen of his urine. ¶ "What's urine?" asked Mike of the doctor, who explained the meaning of the word to him. ¶ Mike left the office, smiling with pride at the knowledge he had gained that day. ¶ The following day, however, he came into the doctor's office with a black eye, a bloody nose and the shirt torn off his back. ¶ "Another one of your Irish brawls," said the doctor. "Well, what's happened to you this time?" ¶ "I was comin' down the street with me little bottle, sayin' nothin' to nobody, when along comes O'Reilly. 'What's that you got in that little bottle,' he says to me. 'That's urine,' says I. 'What?' says he. 'Piss,' says I. 'Shit,' says he. 'Fuck,' says I, and the fight was on."

•44•

Hitler—the dick-taster of Germany.

·45·

A lesbian, alighting from a taxi-cab, in front of a civic repertory theatre, neglected to tip the driver. He insulted her by calling her a cheap little cunt-lapper. She picked up the crank handle, hit him over the head with it and then kicked him around the street until he lay there unconscious in a pool of blood. ¶ A famous actress, who had witnessed the scene, came over to the other lesbian and said, "You ought to be ashamed of yourself. It's your kind who are giving us girls a bad name."

·46·

Three fairies were spending a quiet afternoon at home. During an intermission the first two told the third he ought to do something about the goiter on his neck. He promptly supplied himself with knitting needles and yarn and started to knit baby clothes.

That night while the first two argued over the possession of a mounted policeman, the resourceful and imaginative third disappeared with the cop's horse.

When he got back the horse balked at going with the cop.

The next day before taking up his knitting the fairy went out and purchased a pony's saddle.

·47·

"Judge, I want a divorce from this man, his penis is so small that I get no pleasure from him." ¶ "That's not so, your honor," said the husband. "It's because her vagina is so large that she gets no pleasure from me." ¶ The judge granted the divorce and as they were leaving the court room the ex-wife waved the pinky of her right hand at the ex-husband and said, "Goodbye, dear." ¶ He put both index fingers in his mouth, one on each side, stretched his mouth as large as possible and said, "Goodbye, you dirty bitch."

·48·

"You should make that man of yours pay you when he sleeps wit you." Maizie was advising Liza. ¶ "Why should he pay me when I gets just as much fun out of it as he do," said Liza. ¶ "Well, you foolish woman, my boy-friend pays me every time we fuck together." ¶ Liza thought this proposition over seriously, and when the big six-foot Sammy came to her room the following Saturday night, she said to him. "Look you here feller, I want to be paid if you're goin' to have monkey business wit me tonight." ¶ "Why Liza, I have never paid you before. I thought you liked it." ¶ "I like it well enough, Sammy, but I want to be paid just the same." ¶ "How much do you want woman, how much you want?" ¶ "You just give me what you think I'm worth, that ought to be plenty." ¶ So they went to bed, and Sammy, knowing there was money involved, fucked furiously as the beating rain outside and almost as often as the drops fell rhythmically on the roof. ¶ When Liza woke in the morning, Sam had already left and on the table next to the bed was a nice new shiny dime. ¶ Liza was happy with the world as she walked down the main street on the way to church, humming to herself and smiling from ear to ear. The sun was shining making mirrors of the puddles that remained from the rain of the night before. Liza, stepping off the curbstone had to spread her legs widely and looking down, saw the reflection of her pussy in one of the puddles. She playfully pointed her finger at the reflection and said, "There you are, you little ol' moneymaker."

·49·

A Scotchman went into a whore house and said he could spend no more than three dollars. After much begging and coaxing, one of the girls induced him to spend five. He took her upstairs and began to fuck her in the navel. ¶ "That's not the place," she said, "my hole is further down." ¶ "For five dollars," he answered, "I want a hole of my own."

·50·

Meg meets Mym on the streets of London and says.
"I sye, Mym, does you know 'Arry Brown?'' ¶ "Does
I know 'Arry Brown! Took meself off to a pub the other
night and orders meself a mug of ile. Along comes 'Arry
Brown, tikes me mug of ile and drinks it, tikes me in 'is
arms and kisses me, 'e ups me and 'e downs me, wipes
'is cock on me petticoat and goes off singing, 'Britains
Never Will Be Slives.' Does I know 'Arry Brown!''

·51·

"I say, Tommy." Asked one English soldier of another,
while in the trenches. "What is this transmigration of
souls I've been 'earin' so much about?'' ¶ "Well Bill,
you see it's like this: A German shell comes along and
blows your bloody 'ead off. By the time the war is over
you're covered with mud and dirt. First thing you know
you springs up in the form of a daisy and a cow comes
along, eats you up and shits you out again. Then I comes
strollin' through the field, with Marge on me arm, I sees
this cow flop and I taps it with me walkin' stick and
says, "Hullo Bill ol' boy, why you ain't chinged a bit."

·52·

She was by far the best girl in the whore-house. Often
she would pick up twenty, sometimes forty men in a
night, walk-up the two flights of stairs to her little room
and be better paid than any other girl in the brothel.
Consequently, the madam was greatly surprised when
she tendered her resignation. ¶ "Honey, why are you
quitting?'' asked the madam. "At the rate you're going
you'll be able to retire in a year or two and settle down
to a happy married life." ¶ "I know madam," answered
the whore. "But I can't go on this way. I'm all worn
out and can't stand it any longer." ¶ "I know how it is,
my dear, but why don't you take it a little easy. Cut it
down and only take on about ten men a night for a while."
¶ "It ain't the men that bother me madam. It's those
stairs that are killing me."

·53·

Murphy ran into the doctor's office and Jesus his prick was scratched up to beat old hell. The doctor bandaged him up properly and asked, "Where the hell have you been Murphy?" ¶ "I've been up in Hogan's alley." said Murphy and left. ¶ Next came Riley and bejesus, he was in a worse condition than Murphy. Not only his prick but his balls were scratched and bleeding. The doctor fixed him up and asked. "Where have you been to get scratched up this way, Riley?" ¶ "Shure, and I've been up in Hogan's alley, doctor." ¶ No sooner had he left when in walked Kelly in a worse condition than his two predecessors. His belly, prick and balls were terribly scarred and clawed. After fixing him up the doctor asked him the same question to which he replied, "I've been up in Hogan's alley, Doc. and it's the last time I'll ever go there." ¶ Some time passed when a fourth Irishman walked in, but instead of his prick, his ass-hole and the vicinity were frightfully clawed and bleeding. ¶ "What's your name?" asked the doctor, after treating him. ¶ "Shure, Doc," he answered, "Me name is Hogan."

·54·

"Jack, you've always told me how much you like three way broads. Well, I've just discovered a four way broad down at the new whore house." ¶ "What is the fourth way?" asked Jack. ¶ "She lets you go down on her." was the reply.

·55·

The school teacher had gas on her stomach very badly, and, to save herself the embarrassment of being heard every time she farted, she would shout, "Hurrah for America!" and as the children hurrahed, their noise would drown the sound of the fart. ¶ When she came in one morning, the class was in an uproar. On inquiring the meaning of the noise she was told that little Johnnie shouted, "Hurrah for Cuba," by mistake, and had shit in his pants in the silence that followed.

·56·

An old millionaire proposed marriage to a young and beautiful show-girl. "I am a very passionate woman," she said, "and will only marry you if you draw up a contract promising to fuck me three times every night for a year. If you fail to do this and break the contract, you forfeit one hundred thousand dollars." ¶ The contract was drawn up and they were married. ¶ The millionaire lived up to the agreement for six months, and then, feeling he was about to weaken, went to a doctor for advice. The only thing the doctor could advise was that he soak his prick in extra heavy cream after each fuck, and that would give it new vigor. ¶ The show girl, much surprised to find her husband holding up this long, peeked through the key-hole one night as he was soaking his prick in preparation for the next fuck. ¶ "The son-of-a-bitch," she said. "So that's how he does it. He has a self filler, the old bastard."

·57·

Mandy had a terrific hangover when she walked into the Hanson Drug Store one Sunday morning and asked for a bottle of gin. ¶ "Madam," said the drug clerk politely, "there are three kinds of gin. Bordon's Gin, High and Dry Gin and ordinary every day gin. Which brand do you wish?" ¶ "Man," answered Mandy, "there are three kinds of turd. There's a musturd and there's dog turd and you, you big shit, give me ordinary every day gin."

·58·

A railroad train had rudely interrupted the amorous dalliance of Sam and Mandy, both of whom escaped with their lives but with bruises and broken bones. Mandy was suing the company for damages. ¶ "Tell the court," directed her attorney, "just what happened." ¶ "Well, your honor," Mandy responded. "You see it was like this: I was comin', an' Sam was comin', an' the train was comin', an' none of us could stop!"

An old millionaire proposed marriage.

·59·

Mandy was in court, accused of felonious assault upon the person of Sammy. Sammy, swathed in bandages and hobbling on crutches, looked as if he had picked a quarrel with a rock-crusher. Mandy, he testified, with no provocation whatever, had beaten him unmercifully with a flatiron. The court asked Mandy for her version. ¶ "It was this way, judge your honor," she said. "I was doin' an ironin' an' mindin' my business when this big feller comes along. It was a hot day an' I didn't have on nuthin' but my wrapper. He starts fussin' with me, an' I says 'Go 'long an' leave me be.' But he don't pay no attention, sir. He just keeps feelin' me up. I tells him again to get along about his business, but he just keeps right on foolin' with me. And, well, judge, you know how it is. I'm just human, judge, and finally he got me all hot an' bothered. I pulled up my wrapper, real excited—an', judge, he wasn't ready! He wasn't anymore ready'n you is this minute, judge!"

·60·

Sunday afternoon, Joe is at home watching the football game on T.V. His wife feels neglected and threatens to leave him.

"I'll tell you what," says Joe, not wanting to miss the game or his wife, "Everytime the Giants score a fieldgoal, you can give me a blow job. When they score a touchdown, I'll fuck you."

His wife happily agrees.

The Giants score more points than they have in any game in the previous 3 seasons. Joe and his wife fuck 3 times and she is about to administer her second blow job when Joe stops her.

"No more, I've had enough! The fans just tore down the goalpost!"

·61·

First man: Do you know how to keep an asshole in suspense?
Second man: No, how?
First man: I'll tell you tomorrow.

·62·

Antonio Martinelli wanted to start his daughter and son off right in the world, so he gave them each fifty dollars when they went out to earn their own living. ¶ Every year there was a family re-union of the Martinelli's, and, every year Gloria looked more prosperous, while the son, Frankie, stayed in about the same position with his organ and monkey. ¶ At one of these re-unions, the father was led to inquire of Frankie, "How is ita, Gloria she macka alla da money and you stay a da same way?" ¶ "Well you see Pop; Sis got da cunt, I got da monk: nobody fucka da monk."

·63·

Two young girls were hired to take care of the rectory library. While looking for a book one day, a priest came under the ladder upon which one of the girls was standing putting books in order. He glanced up and seeing the girl without drawers, said, "Here, my good girl, take this two dollars and go out and buy yourself some drawers." ¶ She ran to the other girl, who, after having heard what happened, took off her drawers and got up the ladder under which the priest stood. He glanced up and said, "Here, my dear girl, is a quarter, go out and get yourself a shave."

·64·

A fellow, complaining that he broke through all the different varieties of condrums which the drug clerk had sold him, followed the clerks advice and used two condrums at the same time. The two were no more effective than one had been. On successive nights he came through three, four, and five protectors, worn simultaneously. Determined to stem his virility, he finally adjusted six rain-coats on his tool and went to work. The next day the clerk inquired solicitiously, if the six had done the job. ¶ "I've decided to have a baby. The damn thing back-fired and almost blew my balls off."

·65·

Silas and Hiram, two New England farmers, met one day on the road. ¶ "Hi," said Silas, "I hate to tell yuh, but I don't think your wife is true to yuh." ¶ "Howcum?" demanded Hiram. ¶ "Well, yesttiday," said Silas, "I wuz passin' your place, an' I see that new hired man go into the kitchen an' begin talkin' to your wife, confidential like." ¶ "Yes," said Hiram nervously. "What then?" ¶ "Well, then they sort o' laughed, an' went into the front room." ¶ "Yes," said Hiram. "What then?" ¶ "Then," said Silas, "I'd got past the kitchen, an' from where I wuz walkin' I could see 'em start upstairs." ¶ "Yes," said Hiram, "an' what then?" ¶ "Well," said Silas, "it 'peared to me like I ought to sort o' see what wuz goin' on, so I shinnied up the porch post to the bedroom window. They come into the bedroom an' he began kissin' her." ¶ "Yes," said Hiram, "an' what then?" ¶ "Well, then," said Silas, "they got onto the bed an' began huggin' an' cuddlin' up to each other." ¶ "Yes, yes," said Hiram, "an' what did they do then?" ¶ "Well," said Silas, "I cain't 'xactly rightly tell. Just about that time I had my pleasure an' fell off the roof."

·66·

"Noo Bernie, you're looking very prosperous dese days. Vat you doing for a leeving?" asked Jake of his friend, who he had not seen in years. ¶ "Vell Jake, ven I saw you last time I had nothing, so I borrowed a hundred dollars from Greenspan, bought a horse and now I'm doink fine in de manure business." ¶ "It's a good idea, Bernie, I tink I'll try it myseluf." ¶ They met again about a year later and Bernie asked, "Noo Jake, deed you buy horses and go in de manure business?" ¶ "I deed, Bernie, but it vas no goot." ¶ "Vat vas de matter?" ¶ "Vell, I bought three horses. Effery day I geeve dem oats and hay, and effery night I go into de stable and all dey do iss fart like dis, foof, foof. You know Bernie, a man can't leeve on promises."

·67·

A man, on entering a whore house, was surprised to find a large NRA sign, prominently displayed. He asked the madam the meaning of this patriotic gesture. She replied, "No Rubbers Allowed. We Douche Our Parts."

·68·

A minister, while visiting a lunatic asylum, came to the cell of the patient reputed to be the most unusual in the hospital. ¶ "Why are you in here?" he asked. ¶ "There is really no reason, sir, I was railroaded here, and the way I'm persecuted is simply dreadful, dreadful," he replied. "Why, they follow me around from morn till night erasing." ¶ "Erasing?" asked the minister. "What do you mean erasing?" ¶ "Well, you see sir it's like this. I have a piece of white chalk and a piece of black chalk and everytime I write on the wall with the white chalk they immediately erase it with a black eraser, and when I write with the black chalk they erase it with a white eraser. But I'll fool them yet, in fact I'm ahead of them at the moment. I have a shit and a fuck on the white wall, the picture of a prick on the black wall and I just scribbled cunt on your collar."

·69·

Sammy had just met Liza at a dance that evening and after much coaxing, she acquiesced to let him walk her home. ¶ Sammy was feeling exceptionally romantic on this Spring night and as they strolled along the cow path, he sighed and said, "Some moon, eh honey." ¶ "Yeah Sam, some moon." ¶ He walked to the side of the path where some wild roses were blooming, and said, "Some roses, eh honey." ¶ "Yeah Sam," she answered. "Some roses." ¶ The dew was shining like diamonds on the grass and Sam was led to remark, "Some dew, eh honey." ¶ "Yeah, some do feller, but I don't. Be on your way."

·70·

A wealthy fairy checked in at the Ritz Carlton Hotel. He noticed that bellboy number 7, was particularly fat and handsome and summoned him to his room that night. ¶ "Did you ever drink champagne?" he asked the boy. ¶ "No sir." ¶ "Would you like to try it?" ¶ "Yes sir. I sure would." ¶ "Well you go out and get a few quarts and we'll drink it together." ¶ The boy did as he was bid and they drank champagne until he passed out on the bed. The fairy then took his pants down and gave him the works in the ass. ¶ The following day number 7 asked one of the other boys on the bench, "Did you ever drink champagne, Jack?" ¶ "Yes, I've drunk it many times. Have you?" ¶ "Yes, I drank lots of it last night." ¶ "Do you like it?" ¶ "I like it well enough, but it sure does make your ass-hole hurt the next day," answered number 7.

·71·

Little Willie asked his gray haired old Grandma, "Grandma, will you tell me a story tonight?" ¶ "Yes surely," said grandma laying aside her knitting. "Come, climb on grandma's knee and she will tell you a story. ¶ "Once upon a time there were two fairies and they were sucking one anothers cocks for all they were worth." ¶ "Aw shit, grandma," said Willie, "All your fucking stories begin that way."

·72·

An Indian Chief, returning to his squaw after having been in New York for some time and gotten a taste of metropolitan women, was heard to remark from his tent when they retired that night, "Nice big cigar, smokum, no chewum."

·73·

Quite a party was going on. After the tenth drink or thereabouts everybody was feeling Rosy. Rosy got sore and went home.

·74·

A bachelor sheep farmer migrated out West because there was no work back East. In the Western town, there was work, but no women. After he had been there for about a month, he was pretty horny and consulted a man at the local bar. "We-l-l-l," the man said, "You'll have to do what the rest of us do," and he pointed to the assembled sheep-farming townsmen. "You'll have to make do with a sheep." "Oh, no, I can't possibly do that," the Easterner said, and he returned to his ranch unsatisfied. A month later, by this time sexually desperate, he came back into town, got roaring drunk, and went out into the night and grabbed the first sheep he could find. It was not as bad as he expected, so he swaggered back into the bar, leading the sheep behind him. An immediate and ominous silence fell on the assembled throng, as they gazed as one on the newcomer. Stunned by his reception, he asked his benefactor, "What's wrong?" "You damn fool," he said, "You've got the sheriff's girlfriend!"

·75·

A young and beautiful woman was in bed anxiously waiting for her lover to disrobe so that he might join her. "Oh hurry dear, I want so much to be with you." ¶ He slowly pulled off his necktie saying without enthusiasm, "Yeh, I'll be there." ¶ "What's the matter darling, you used to be so anxious to come to me. Are you tired?" ¶ He slowly took off his vest and his shirt saying, "No I'm all right—" ¶ "Darling I want you so—" ¶ At this moment there was a tremendous banging on the door. "What's that?" said the lover. ¶ "My God, it's my husband." ¶ Upon hearing this the man threw off the rest of his clothes and leaped onto the bed on top of her. ¶ "What's the matter with you? Are you crazy?" ¶ "No, everything's O.K. now. I'm scared stiff."

·76·

The latest definition of a Virgin. A dame that doesn't give a fuck.

·77·

A woman, having won the worlds wrestling championship, was making a tour of the country, giving exhibitions in wrestling and offering a thousand dollars to anyone, male or female, who could stay in the ring with her for three minutes. ¶ The prize had never been won as very few people dared to enter the ring against the huge amazon, and those who had tried were quickly defeated. One night, in Kansas City, a little anaemic looking fellow stepped up to the ring and offered to take her on. The crowd was in an uproar and the amazon's manager warned the little fellow that she would probably break his back in the first minute. But as he was willing to take the risk, they fixed him up with trunks and he entered the ring amid the guffaws of the vast audience. ¶ The gong rang and they were in the middle of the ring tussling, but not for long, as, in a flash the little fellow had her flat on the mat. He had won the bout, the thousand dollars, and the world's championship. ¶ He was carried to his dressing room on the shoulders of the frenzied fans, where newspaper men besieged him with cameras and questions. "How did you do it?" they all asked. ¶ "I used the bowling hold," the little fellow said.

·78·

An Irishman brought his brother over from Ireland, and the green-horn, on the day of his arrival, took out his prick on Broadway and pissed in front of everyone. His brother told him that that sort of thing was not done here. "If you have to piss, go to any house, knock on the door, and they'll let you use the toilet." ¶ Early the following morning, the green-horn had to piss again. He went up to a bungalow and knocked on the door. ¶ The door opened and a hand came out with a tin receptacle accompanied by fifteen cents and a voice that said, "One quart, please." ¶ When he saw his brother later that day, he said, "Jesus, Pat, why didn't you bring me over here sooner. I pissed away a fortune in the old country."

·79·

The odds were three to one that Bigballsky "The Bone Crusher" would easily throw Hung Too Low, the champion of all China, in the championship bout that night. Bigballsky was in better shape than he had been when he threw Kant Ake It the Japanese champ and there wasn't much doubt that he would easily win tonight's bout. ¶ The first few minutes in the ring he was mopping up the mat with Hung Too Low, throwing him around with slight effort and having altogether what seemed a cinch, when suddenly, without apparent reason, he stretched out on his back with a moan and it was all over. ¶ "What happened?" demanded his manager, when he revived in the dressing room. ¶ "Remember," said the ex-champ, "When we were all tied up in knots, my ass in his face, his ass in mine? Well, one of his balls slipped through the leg of his trunks and dangled in front of my mouth." ¶ "Why the hell didn't you bite it?" asked the manager. ¶ "I did," said the erstwhile wrestler, "And it was my own ball."

·80·

"Judge, I want a divorce from that man I'm married to," said Daisy. ¶ "What is your reason for wanting a divorce, Daisy?" ¶ "Well, Judge your honor, that man has me ten times a night." ¶ "Daisy, I'm sorry, but I can't give you a divorce on those grounds." ¶ "Wait, your honor, then he goes and has my poor old mother a few times." ¶ "Why, Daisy, for that I can send the rascal to jail." ¶ "Wait a minute, Judge. Then he goes and has my poor old grandmother." ¶ "I'll give him life for that, Daisy." ¶ "But, wait, Judge, you ain't heard nothing yet. He then goes and has my poor little ten-year-old sister." ¶ "I can and I will send him to the electric chair for that." ¶ "Wait, your honor, you ain't heard nothing yet. Then he gets his glasses, puts them on that big hard-on of his and says, "Come on, boy, look around and see if there's anything you've missed."

·81·

"I saw your sign outside, Rhyming Waiter Wanted, and if you explain the meaning of it, to me, perhaps I can fill the position." ¶ "Well you see," said the owner of the restaurant, "there have been dancing waiters and singing waiters, and I think the novelty of having a rhyming waiter would help my business considerably." ¶ "I was a poet once and I think I can fill the job," said the applicant. ¶ "I'll try you out, but if you can't rhyme the orders as you get them, I'll have to fire you." ¶ The first customers the new waiter had, were two Jewish men, who ordered two stews. They were followed by a whore with red shoes who ordered the same. Next came an innocent looking country girl, who ordered two soft boiled eggs in a glass. ¶ The waiter shouted the three orders in this manner:
"Two stews, for two Jews,
The same for a whore with red shoes,
Two eggs in a glass, for a country lass,
And if that doesn't rhyme, I'll kiss your ass."

·82·

Mrs. Mefufsky went to the lower east side to make some purchases. Amongst the things she bought were a half dozen bananas. Before she arrived at the Bronx subway train she had lost five of the six, so, to safeguard the remaining one she put it under her dress and held it tightly. The train was crowded and she had to stand up. ¶ When half way home, a man standing in front of her said, "All right madam, you may let go of it now. I have to get off at this station."

·83·

A pigeon invited all of his friends to fly over to the top of the Empire State Building and when they got there, he strutted out to the end of a flag pole and answered nature's call. Ten pairs of eyes watched the offering twist and twirl its way to the street below. "I just wanted to show you how far a little shit will go in this town."

·84·

"Judge, I want a divorce from this man," said Matilda. ¶ "What is your reason for wanting to divorce him, Matilda?" asked the judge. ¶ "I don't get no satisfaction from him, that's the reason." ¶ "Tell the court the reason he doesn't satisfy you," ordered the judge. ¶ "I can't tell any reason, judge. You better see for yourself." ¶ So the judge ordered the puny little husband to take down his pants. Down they came, revealing an instrument of prodigious length and thickness. The astonished judge pointed to the tool and said, "You mean to say, Matilda, that this fellow can't satisfy you with *that*?" ¶ "That's right, judge. Tell him to turn around." ¶ The husband turned his back to the court as he was ordered and there were displayed two tiny black buttocks, about the size of a child's. ¶ "You see," said Matilda, "You can't expect to drive a spike with a tack hammer."

·85·

"Keep to the right"—"Keep to the right" ordered the usher as a large crowd of people arrived at the theatre. One rather busty woman disregarded the usher's request completely. ¶ The boy went to the woman and said in a most persuasive tone, "Please keep to the right madam." ¶ Even then the woman paid no attention. ¶ Finally he tapped her on the arm and again asked her to keep to the right. In an indignant manner she said, "Young man, I'll have you know I have a mezzanine box." ¶ "Lady, I don't care if you have brass tits, keep to the right," he answered.

·86·

A girl rode up to the village postoffice on a bicycle, leaned the bike against the curb, and dismounted. As she entered the postoffice the bicycle toppled over. ¶ "Your wheel seems to be a bit tired," the old postmaster remarked. The girl retorted: ¶ "You'd be tired too, if you'd been between my legs as long as that wheel has."

·87·

The red-headed senator from Illinois got into a controversy with the senator from Ohio.

Said the senator from Illinois:
> "Here's to the American eagle
> A great and glorious bird
> That flew all over the union
> And in Ohio dropped a turd."

Said the senator from Ohio:
> "Here's to the state of Ohio
> Who's soil is fertile and rich
> Which needs no turd from your old bird
> You red-headed son-of-a-bitch!"

·88·

A prostitute went to the bank to deposit a twenty dollar bill. The clerk looked it over and said, "Mazie, you've been fucked. This bill is no good." ¶ "Fucked," she yelled, "I've been raped."

·89·

A chap was convalescing from an operation in the hospital and the continued presence of a nurse in his room annoyed him. One night he said to the nurse, "Would you mind stepping out into the corridor for a few minutes?" ¶ "Why?" she asked, "What do you wish to do?" ¶ "I'm embarrassed, nurse, I have to do something very badly and I'd rather be alone." ¶ "But you must tell me what it is. You shouldn't be ashamed of anything you have to do in front of me." ¶ "Well, I am, and I won't do it until you leave the room." ¶ "Oh come now, tell me what it is. Do you have to belch?" ¶ "No. Something much worse than that." ¶ "Do you have to piss?" ¶ "Nope." ¶ "Do you have to shit?" ¶ "No." ¶ "Do you have to fart, then?" ¶ "Yes nurse that's it, I have to break wind." ¶ "Well you shouldn't be ashamed of that, everytime you break wind it's a feather in my cap." ¶ "Well," he said, "If that's the way you feel about it, stand over there against the wall and I'll make an Indian Chief out of you."

·90·

Two fellows, after graduating from an Ivy League college, decided they had a scheme in mind whereby they could clean up thousands of dollars. They carved a wooden prick and painted it so that it looked for all the world like the real thing. Then they went to McGurk's speakeasy and sat in the back room. ¶ One of the best customers in the establishment came to McGurk and said, "Mac, I've been a friend of yours for a long time, as well as your best customer. But little did I ever suspect that you would allow this sort of thing to go on in your place." ¶ "What sort of thing are you referring to?" asked McGurk. ¶ "Why, those fairies in the back room, and one sucking the other's cock right out in the open." ¶ "You're crazy, man, I never had a fairy in this place." ¶ "I'll bet you fifty dollars there are two of them in there right now." ¶ "You're on," said McGurk. ¶ They went into the back room and sure enough there was one fellow sucking the other fellow's cock. McGurk put them both out and they met the best customer later who split the fifty dollars with them. ¶ For a month the scheme had been working very successfully. No more trivial bets like fifty dollars for the boys. Now they were working the high class places where the bets ran into thousands. ¶ One night they came into Rosenberg's place on Park Avenue. Rosenberg had never lost a bet in his life, and bet his best customer five thousand dollars that no such thing could be going on in his place, but sure enough he lost the bet. ¶ That night the two college boys were talking things over when the boy who did the sucking said, "I think that damned wooden prick needs re-painting or something. All the shellac came off in my mouth tonight." ¶ "Shellac hell," the other answered, "I had to slip you the real thing. That guy was far too clever."

·91·

Practice makes pregnant.

·92·

All the animals at the Bronx zoo were given a night off to go to Broadway and raise hell. The condition made by the keeper was that they were all to be back at ten o'clock that night. Ten o'clock arrived and all had returned but the Giraffe and the Monkey. At twelve o'clock the Giraffe came in looking very bedraggled and worn out from her escapade. The keeper bawled her out properly and sent her to bed. At two-thirty in the morning, Mr. Monkey came staggering along looking most dissipated and more bedraggled than the Giraffe had looked. "Where have you been?" inquired the keeper. "I thought you were told to be back here by ten o'clock?" ¶ "I've been out with Miss Giraffe, keeper." ¶ "Why even Miss Giraffe arrived here over two hours ago." ¶ "Well sir, between kissing her and screwing her, I wore myself completely out."

·93·

A Frenchman and an American were having an argument, during which the American called the Frenchman a cock-sucker. ¶ "Sometimes," replied the Frenchman, "In ze heat of passion I kiss ze pussy. But suck ze cock, nevair!"

·94·

A chap, who stuttered uncontrollably, took a position as clerk in a book store. The first day a woman came in and asked for Charles Dicken's "A Tale of Two Cities." When the clerk repeated this it was "A Sale of Two Tities." The woman left the store horrified. Never in her life had she been so insulted. The clerk was warned that the next time anything like this happened he would be dismissed. ¶ The following day an old lady came in, and talked with the clerk for a moment. He went to the proprietor and said, "I wish to resign my position." ¶ "What's the trouble?" asked the owner. ¶ "This lady wants a book called "Friar Tuck."

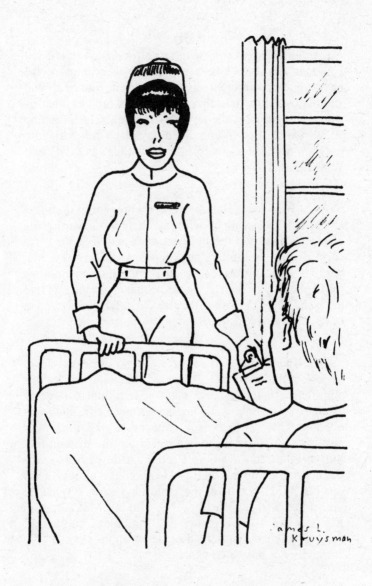

The continued presence of a nurse annoyed him.

36

·95·

Spending a week-end with some friends our guest felt a sudden desire to take a shit in the wee hours of the morning. Not wanting to disturb anyone he looked around and deposited his package in a hat box thinking that he would dispose of it the next day. Completely forgetting about it he left for home. Two days later he received a telegram from his host which read: "ALL IS FORGIVEN. WHERE IS IT?"

·96·

A condrum manufacturer went to a broadcasting station and asked, "How much will you charge to advertise my condrums between the hours of five and six?" ¶ "I'm sorry sir, but the sanitary napkin people already have that hour," he was informed. ¶ "I'll pay a thousand dollars for the hour." he said. ¶ Those people are paying us five thousand." ¶ "Yes, but they're out after blood. We're only out after pleasure."

·97·

One by one the girls of the whore house came down to look at the prick of 'Conceited Al', and one by one admired it, but refused to take on anything as large as all that. ¶ The only girl who had not been consulted was a whore who was kept there only for an occasional poor customer. Al insisted on being laid, so the madam told him to go up to the whore's room and force her to take the huge prick up her cunt. ¶ He entered the room, took out his prick, put it on the table, and said, "What do you think of that, Maizie?" ¶ "Mmmm Mmmm, man it's just like a stove pipe." ¶ "Big, huh?" he asked, feeling satisfied that he had made an impression. ¶ "No man, dirty," answered Maizie.

·98·

Two fairies were having an argument when one said to the other, "You kiss my ass." ¶ The other said, "This is a fight, dearie, don't bring romance into it."

·99·

A tramp had been trying all the homes in Westchester for a hand out, but to no avail. All the women were far too elegant to help out a poor starving tramp. However, he finally came to a house where the woman invited him in and prepared an elegant meal, which she served herself. As she was dressed only in a negligee, each time she bent over to serve a course, the tramp could not help but see her breasts and several times her hairy cunt. Consequently, all during the meal he had an erection, which insisted on showing itself through the various holes in his trousers. Each time it popped out he would push it back, only to have it come through another aperture. ¶ That night at the bridge club, the ladies of Westchester were discussing the day's happenings. "A terrible tramp came to my door today, but I chased him away with a broom stick," said one. ¶ "Was he a tall husky, raggedy fellow?" asked another. "Why he's the same beast I chased away myself." ¶ "Did he have red hair?" asked the philanthropic lady who had fed the tramp. ¶ "Yes," all the others answered in unison. "The beast did have red hair." ¶ "Well," said our great souled friend, "I've never seen a beast with so many cocks before in my life."

·100·

"Doctor I want you to look me over." ¶ The doctor made a cursory examination. "Well," he said, "from what I observe, you have one of two things. Either a very bad cold or a slight touch of syphilis." ¶ "My God doctor, don't you know, I've come to you for a diagnosis?" ¶ "I shall know very exactly after I've made some tests," said the M.D. and went into his laboratory. ¶ He came back and put his hand on the man's shoulder. "Now don't get nervous and excited," he said, "but I have to report that you have syphilis." ¶ "Well of course, doctor," said the patient, "where the hell would I catch a cold?"

·101·

A Roumanian Princess was searching all over the country for the man with the biggest prick. When she found this man, she would marry him and make him the Prince. After she had searched near and far without finding the right man, she was told of three brothers who lived in a small province and were the possessors of huge tools, the hugest belonging to the brother named Marchand. ¶ She came upon one of the three in the orchard, who was very busy knocking olives from a tree with his cock. "You must be Marchand," she said, "and you shall be my husband." ¶ But he said, "I am not Marchand, you will find him over in the fields plowing." ¶ She went to the field and there was another brother, plowing the fields and using his prick as the plow. She embraced him, and cried, "Oh Marchand, at last I have found you." ¶ But he replied, "Lady, you must be mistaken. You will find Marchand on the other side of that river." ¶ She mounted her beautiful white horse and proceeded to the river. Standing on the other bank was a man with his back turned. "Yoo hoo," called the princess. "Where can I find Marchand?" ¶ "I am Marchand." a voice came back. ¶ "How shall I get over there to you?" ¶ Marchand turned around and his prick bridged the two banks, whereupon the princess and her horse rode over and they lived happily ever after.

·102·

A Chinaman bought a thousand dollar bond, which dropped to nine hundred and fifty the following day. He rushed to his broker who calmed him with, "Don't get excited. You see bond prices fluctuate, the price of yours will probably go up again soon." ¶ The following day the price dropped to nine hundred, and the Chinaman again ran furiously to the broker, who again explained. "I told you the prices fluctuate. Just hold on, it will come back." ¶ "Oh," said the Chinaman, "Me savvy, flucked again!"

·103·

Three Scotchmen were riding on a train from Edinburgh to Glasgow. Sandy, who was sitting opposite them, noticed that every now and then they took out a bottle and passed it along the line, each one of the three putting it to his lips. Finally Sandy got up enough courage to ask, "What say, me laddies, whoo aboot passin' that bottle to Sandy?" ¶ Without hesitation, they passed the bottle to him. He was surprised to find it almost full, but knowing the proverbial stinginess of Scots, he took a good long drink, and offered back the bottle. ¶ "Therres no hurry me laddie," said one of the three. "Keep it forr a while longer if you wish." ¶ "Sandy was amazed at such generosity from his countrymen and took another big swig from the bottle. ¶ "What kinda stuff is this you'rre a drinkin' me good lads? It's verra good but in me life I neverr tasted it beforre." ¶ "It's nothin' to drink, lad. We'rre three consumptives and 'ave been spitting our blood into tha' bootle since we left Edinburgh."

·104·

Two cockneys met at a public urinal. "What's the first symptoms of syphilis 'Arry?" ¶ "I don't know Alf. Why?" ¶ "Me cock just came off in me 'ands."

·105·

A large and a small Irishman were passing through the muddy streets of a mining town. They were attracted by sounds of ribaldry coming from a honky-tonk. ¶ "Let's go in and get a drink," said the little one. ¶ "I wouldn't do that, me boy, it's a tough joint that is," said the bigger fellow. ¶ "Tough joint or not, I'm goin' in." And the little one entered the honky-tonk. Scarcely a minute passed when he came flying out of the window and landed like a ball in the mud. ¶ "Wasn't I after tellin' ye it was a tough joint?" asked the big one. ¶ "Sure and a tough joint it is. But will you tell me one thing. Whose balls are these I have in me hand?"

·106·

Johnnie was annoyed by the fact that every afternoon as he lay in the grass he would get a terrible erection. He went to the blacksmith, who was his friend and told him of this condition. The blacksmith put Johnnie's prick on the anvil, struck it a mighty blow with his sledge and lo and behold the erection was gone. After that Johnnie went to the smithy every day to have his prick hit with the sledge. ¶ One day when he arrived, the blacksmith was not at the shop and Johnnie ran to his home expecting to find him there. The smithy's wife answered the knock at the door and inquired if there was anything she could do as her husband was not at home. He told her about the hard-on and she promptly took him inside and let him fuck her. ¶ The next day, as Johnnie was running past the shop, the blacksmith came up and said, "Where are you running to Johnnie, don't you want me to fix your hard-on?" ¶ "Naw, I'm going to see your wife, she fixes it so that it hurts nice."

·107·

"Papa," said little Willie, "You were a sheep herder in your younger days, perhaps you can tell me where virgin wool comes from." ¶ "Virgin wool, my son, comes from the sheep the herders couldn't catch."

·108·

A farmer got an order for four dozen chickens. Upon going out to the coops he found he had only forty seven. He decided to use the parrot in place of the missing chicken. The forty eight were loaded on the wagon, and about a mile away from town, the forty seven chickens were walking on the road in back of the wagon and the parrot was standing on the running board. He shouted, "If any of you girls change your minds, let me know and you can ride."

·109·

Little Junior was taken by his mother to a big toy department just before Christmas. There he indulged himself fully. He shot the chutes and he slid the slides and he galloped the hobbyhorse despite his mother's urgent request that he come home; for it was getting late and dinner would soon be ready. To all this Junior turned a deaf ear. He was having the time of his life and there wouldn't be much toy department left after he got through with it. His mother turned to the furred and whiskered Santa Claus always provided by stores on such occasions. "Would you mind," she said, "telling my Junior that he must come with me at once?" He thinks you're the real Santa Claus, and you might help me out." ¶ "Of course," said Santa. "I shall be glad to assist you." Whereupon he went over to the boy and whispered a few words in his ear. Immediately Junior leaped off the horse and ran to his mother saying "I'm ready, Mummy. I'll go home." ¶ In the street his mother asked him what it was that Santa had said to make him so obedient. Junior's lip trembled but he wouldn't say. "Did he tell you that if you were a good boy and went with Mummy he'd bring you lots of presents for Christmas?" ¶ Junior shook his head in the negative. "No, Mummy. He didn't say anything about presents." ¶ "Then what did he say, darling?" asked his mother. ¶ "He said, 'you little cock-sucking sonofabitch, if you don't get off that horse this minute, I'll kick the piss out of you!' "

·110·

Mr. Perkins was sitting in the hospital awaiting word of a blessed event. The nurse arrived and told him that he was the proud father of twins. Much elated he started for the door. ¶ "Mr. Perkins," called the nurse, "a third one has arrived." ¶ "A Ahem," said Mr. Perkins, "before I leave do you mind looking around a bit? You know she was always a pretty roomy sort of a girl."

·111·

"Boys," said a tramp as he entered a saloon. "I must have a drink. My nerves are shattered and I'll do anything you say for a shot." ¶ "Alright, I'll give you a drink," said the bar-tender. "But if your prick is not as long as that cats tail, you'll have to suck the cunt of Nellie The Bar-Rag, on top of the bar so that everyone may see you." ¶ The tramp looked at Nellie The Bar-Rag, who had passed out in the corner, amongst spitoons, cigar and cigarette butts. He had seen many filthy trollops in his time, but none who could compare with Nellie for sheer disgust. Regardless of the consequences, he gulped down the proffered drink. ¶ The boys were already beginning to drag Nellie over the bar, so sure were they that he would lose the bet. He insisted, however, that they measure the cats tail, which they announced, was ten inches long. They then measured his prick, which, alas, was only seven and a half inches in length. ¶ "From where to where," he inquired, "did you measure the cats tail?" ¶ "Why from his ass-hole to the tip, of course." ¶ "Then in all fairness, I insist that you measure my prick the same way."

·112·

A doctor was asked by a male patient whether it was harmful to masturbate. The doctor replied yes and no— it depends upon the frequency with which the practice is carried out. ¶ "How about three times a day doctor?" ¶ This took the physician aback. "I should say that is altogether too much," he replied. "Is this your daily practice?" ¶ "Yes, three times a day, every day," said the patient. ¶ "Why don't you get yourself a girl?" said the doctor. ¶ "I've got a girl." ¶ "I mean a girl you can live with, sleep with. Who loves you to be with her." ¶ "I got one like that, I'm telling you." ¶ "Then why in heaven's name do you masturbate three times a day?" ¶ "Oh," said the man disgustedly, "She don't like it during meals."

·113·

A Hollywood producer wired his New York representative to the affect that the show "The Captive" had been running in New York for six months now. Why, he wished to know, hadn't it been signed up for his movie company? ¶ The representative wired back: "Can't use the show for movies. All about Lesbians." ¶ To which the producer answered: "Sign it up anyway. We'll make Italians of them and use it."

·114·

The lumber-camp barroom was closing for the night, and the six-foot barkeep was tidying up the back bar, when he felt what seemed to be an earth tremor. The door burst open, and through it came the biggest, toughest-looking man he ever saw. The newcomer was leading a huge bear by a chain. The bear rushed at the bartender, but the big man jerked the chain, and gave the animal a terrible kick, and admonished him: ¶ "Behave yourself, you lousy bastard, or I'll tear your goddam guts out." ¶ The bear cringed and slunk down by the rail. ¶ "Gimme," said the man to the pop-eyed bartender, "a pint of alcohol—straight." ¶ The barkeep poured the alcohol with trembling hands, and the customer gulped it down. At that moment a big rattlesnake thrust out its head from within the drinker's shirt and made as if to attack the now half-paralyzed bartender. The newcomer seized the snake's neck with one hand and crashed his other fist against its head. "Back where you belong," he growled, "or I'll wring your goddam neck." ¶ The snake slid back into his shirt. ¶ "Another pint of whiskey—straight," the customer ordered. ¶ He drank it, and paid. By this time the barkeep was beginning to recover his speech. ¶ "Stranger," he managed to get out, "I guess where you come from, men is men—eh?" ¶ "Where I come from," the customer replied, "they'r so goddam tough that yesterday they chased all us fairies out!"

·115·

A certain movie director was supposed to have married a former Follies girl under the impression that she was a virgin. The basis for his belief was the fact that she took very short steps, and he figured that was caused by the tightness of those secret parts. It was only after his marriage that he discovered she had been fucked so much during her career that she took short steps to keep her insides from falling out!

·116·

The president of a French academy made an official visit to America in order to study conditions. On his return he gave the scholarly report of his findings to the learned members of the board. ¶ "I meet ze beautiful American madame and tell her I must have ze body. While I wait for her entrance in ze chamber, I have ze urge to make ze beeg sheet. I find no water closet so I remove ze socks and sheet in zem. Just zen ze madame come in and I put ze socks in ze coat pocket. ¶ "I say madame, I must have ze body, but she say no, no, no, no, first you must prove ze test of love; you must kiss ze titie. Ah, madam, I say, I love ze titie. ¶ "So after I kiss ze titie I say, madam now ze body. But she say no, no, no, no, zat is only ze first test of love, now you must kiss ze cunt. ¶ "I say to her, madam, I am ze Frenchman. I love ze cunt. After ze cunt is kissed I say, madam I must have ze body now. But she say no, no, no, no, zat is only the second test of love. She say, now you must kiss ze ass. ¶ "Gentlemen of ze French academy, I have nevair kissed ze ass, so I say madam I cannot do zat. But now gentlemen, I have much passion and must have ze body, so I, ze president of zees academy, go on ze knees to kiss ze ass of madam. But ze madam let go ze fart in my face and she say, 'Zat for France!' ¶ "So I pull out ze socks and fling zem in her face and say, 'Viva La France.'"

·117·

The celebrated Mike and Pat were out of a job like many others. Mike saw an advertisement calling for men at the Empire State Tower. On their arrival they were informed that they were expected to demonstrate a new pair of wings that make man the equal of a bird. ¶ Pat the gamer of the two had the wings adjusted, took off from the Tower and had a grand time flying around. After making a perfect landing he asked Mike to try the wings. ¶ Mike was very timid but agreed to try them on condition that Pat go downstairs and stand ready to catch him in case of mishap. Mike took off and was going fine, when something happened to the wings and down he came. ¶ A street cleaner had just finished making a perfect mound and Mike landed head first into the pile. Pat ran over, took one look at Mike and then exploded "I knew god dammed well you couldn't be a bird for two minutes without sticking your head in the horseshit."

·118·

As he was entering his hotel room, he saw his ex-wife, whom he had divorced a year ago going into the next room. He hadn't been fucked since then and was pretty hard up for a piece at the moment, so he knocked on the door of the room she had entered and said, "Let me come in, I'm going to lay you tonight." ¶ "No you're not," she answered. "And what's more you can't come in here." ¶ "Well I'm coming in there if it's the last thing I do." ¶ "If you come in here and lay me it will be over my dead body." ¶ "You're telling me? It was always that way anyhow."

·119·

A whore accosted a young fellow on the street and asked, "How would you like to come upstairs with me?" ¶ "I'd like very much to, but there are three reasons why I can't." ¶ "What are the reasons," she asked. ¶ "Well, the first is that I have no money." ¶ "Good-bye," she said. "You can stick the other two up your ass."

·120·

An American actress rushed out of a London hotel, called a cab and instructed the cabby to take her to the theatre in a hurry. The cabby started off at his usual leisurely pace. She again told him she was in a hurry. ¶ "Yes mum. Come Dobbins!" A short sprint followed and again the horse slowed down. ¶ "Say, cabby, can't you do something to make that animal move faster?" ¶ "No lidy, you see I must save his balls for the hills."

·121·

"Didja ever suck a cunt Johnnie?" ¶ "Naw, did you?" ¶ "Naw, but I know what it tastes like." ¶ "How do you know?" ¶ "Me mother saves all her old drawers for a month and then boils 'em up for soup."

·122·

"Hmmm, and vat do you tink of dis younger generation, Mrs. Feitelbaum? My son Louie, he vants to marry yet, a goy and he vants to be a goy heemself. Yesterday I found heem in de toilet putting new skin, vat they sell in de drug stores, on his prick."

·123·

Zeke was telling the boys on the corner about his wedding night. "Boys, is that girl I married dumb, boy is she dumb. Imagine, instead of putting the pillow under her head when we goes to bed, she puts it under her ass. Boy, is she a dumb woman."

·124·

Chinese words for pussy: Tung chow.
Chinese words for bad pussy: Tung chow yuk.

"She puts it under her ass."

·125·

While riding on a slow train in Montana, I was fascinated by watching the strange antics of a fellow passenger who sat opposite me. At irregular intervals he would pull vigorously on a string which dangled from the back of his shirt collar, while he mumbled some imprecation, which I could not hear. Finally my curiosity got the best of me and after the usual exchange of small talk, I made bold enough to ask the meaning of his strange behavior. He related the following, without hesitation. ¶ About a year ago I found myself stranded in the desert twenty miles outside of the city of Billings. I made my way to a lonely ranch and asked for food. The owner would feed me only on condition that I work for him. Thus, I became a sheep-herder. ¶ My sexual needs became more and more urgent, for there were no women anywhere near this ranch, until I was forced to adopt the custom of the country, ie., find what satisfaction I could in the sheep under my care. I got so that every time I was horny at least two or three of the little dears would prance toward me, nuzzling and rubbing against my legs in their desire to be favored. ¶ You must understand that I am by nature an extremely passionate man and could find little relief in such bucolic pastimes. It was, therefore, with a feeling of keen anticipation that after six months I left the ranch and made my way to Kansas City. Having fallen heir to a small inheritance, I registered at one of the better hotels and prepared myself for a long awaited screw. ¶ A bellboy, properly tipped, brought as beautiful a woman as I had ever set eyes on into my room. ¶ The long awaited moment had arrived. The woman lay naked and willing before me. I need not tell you how alluring she was, nor how the heated blood distended my penis to its full nine inches. My long awaited dream was about to become a reality. ¶ Whether it was my experience with the sheep, whether it was my long period of abstinence from a woman, whether it was some psychological quirk thrusting itself up from my self conscious, whatever it was, the sad fact remains that at this most opportune moment my prick wilted and died just as I was about to insert it. ¶ From that night on every time I think of this devastating experience, I jerk the string and make the son-of-a-bitch kiss my ass.

·126·

A fellow picked up a whore lady on the street and went up to her room with her. ¶ "I only have fifty cents," said he. "What can you give me for that?" ¶ "I'm sorry, sir, but I'm a union girl and we have nothing to give for fifty cents." ¶ "How much does the union make you charge for a lay?" ¶ "Two dollars, sir." ¶ "Would you piss in this pot for fifty cents?" ¶ "Yes sir, that I'll do." ¶ When she had pissed in the pot he took out his prick, swished it around in the piss and said, "Take soup, you son-of-a-bitch, meat's too damned expensive."

·127·

The Virgin Mary got permission of St. Peter, to go on a little visit to Broadway. His only condition was that she return before twelve o'clock, at which time the pearly gates would be closed. ¶ At four A.M., she returned from her escapade looking much the worse for wear. Loudly she knocked on the pearly gates demanding admission. ¶ "This is the Virgin Mary," she called. ¶ "Oh yeah?" said the voice of St. Peter.

·128·

Mr. Hawkins an Englishman was entertaining a guest for the week-end. In the morning the guest walked into the bathroom and much to his embarrassment he found Mrs. Hawkins taking her bath. He immediately rushed out and found Mr. Hawkins. "I am terribly sorry sir, you see it was not my fault the door was open and I walked in and found your wife sitting in the bath tub." Mr. Hawkins calmly twirled his moustache and said, "skinny bitch, eh?"

·129·

Father, mother and daughter had just finished the evening meal when the distressing question of washing the dishes came up. Everyone of them abhorred this task. Finally they agreed that the first one to utter a sound would have to do the dishes. Silence prevailed. ¶ The daughter's young man arrived and greeted the family with his usual boisterous "Hello everybody." ¶ A slight grunt was the only reply. This continued for some time to every remark he made. He couldn't understand it, but started to fondle his sweetheart. Still no sound was heard. He became a little bolder with no admonition from anyone. He decided to fuck her which he did. More grunts from Ma and Pa but nothing said. ¶ He had always had a peculiar yen for the old lady so decided this was as good a time as any to fuck her. Loud grunts came this time from the old man but no interference. The young man rather well satisfied with himself nonchalantly lit a cigar, but in doing so burned his finger. He yelled out loudly "Jesus Christ, have you any vaseline?" Then the old man piped up "Don't give it to the bastard. I'll wash the fucken dishes."

·130·

A circus was parading through a small town; lions, tigers, and nineteen elephants each holding the other's tail in its mouth. As they were crossing the railroad tracks the smallest elephant, and leader of the procession, was struck by a train and killed. ¶ The circus manager sued the railroad company for fifty thousand dollars damages. ¶ The railroad company's lawyer was telling the judge: "Your honor, I can't see why these people are sueing for such a tremendous amount of money. The elephant we killed was the smallest of the lot and certainly no elephant is worth that much money." ¶ "But, your honor," said the lawyer for the circus. "When the railroad train killed little Fifi, it pulled the ass-holes out of the eighteen other elephants."

·131·

A Frenchman and an American were arguing about the number of ways of fucking. The American knew one hundred and one ways, whereas the Frenchman knew only one hundred. They decided to tell each other the various ways each knew. ¶ "The first way," said the American, "Is the conventional manner, whereby the man lays on top of the woman, inserts his prick into her cunt and works up and down until he comes." ¶ "Aha!" said the Frenchman, "That's the only way I didn't know of."

·132·

Having been away to sea for four months, Captain Taylor was pretty hard up for a piece of cunt, and was happy when a woman sidled up to him on the dark street and inquired, "How about a bit of nasty, baby?" ¶ "Alright," said he, "I ain't had a bit of nasty in four months and it would go fine. What's your price?" ¶ "Price ain't me object, captain, I does it for pleasure. But if you want to throw a piece of change me way when you're finished, I won't object one bit." ¶ They walked until they reached a street lamp and Captain Taylor paused to get a better look at the slut he was going to fuck in a short while. ¶ "Here's a hallway," said she, "I guess that's as good a place as any to do a bit of fucking." ¶ "I don't mind hallways," he said, "but you're a homely old hag and I'd like to give you a little feel to work meself up, if you has no objections." ¶ "I has no objections, captain, you go right ahead and feel me up all you wants to." ¶ He started to feel, and suddenly gave her a shove against the wall and shouted, "Why, you son-of-a-bitch you're a man. I've a good mind to beat your head off." ¶ "But captain," she protested, "I ain't a man, feel me tits." ¶ "I don't want to feel your tits, I just felt your god damned prick dangling under that dress you're wearing." ¶ "Prick indeed," she replied indignantly, "Since when, may I ask, can't a lady shit in her own drawers."

·133·

It was the first day of school and the teacher was taking the names of her pupils. Sitting in the first row was a puny little fellow whose name was Percivald Smith, and a few aisles away, also in the first row, another weak looking individual whose name was Reginald Smith. ¶ "Are you and Percivald brothers?" inquired the teacher. ¶ "We're twins mam." answered Reginald. ¶ The teacher came to the back of the room and there crouched a big husky bully whose name was Patrick Smith. ¶ "Are you related to the other Smith boys?" asked the teacher. ¶ "Sure," he replied, "We're triplets." ¶ "How is it they are such nice little fellows and you're such a big overgrown clown?" ¶ "Well you see teacher, me old lady only had two tits and I had to suck on the old man's cock."

·134·

A German captain caught one of the soldiers in the act of taking a shit near the entrance of the fort. The captain seized the private's gun and ordered him to eat the shit. When he had eaten a part of it, the captain said, "That will do," and returned the gun to him. ¶ The private in a rage, leveled the gun at the captain, and said, "Now you eat the rest." ¶ After doing so, the captain rushed to the general and preferred charges. ¶ "What did you do to offend the captain?" asked the general of the private. ¶ "Nothing your worship. We just dined together."

·135·

A young fellow was receiving treatment from a G.U. man (clap doctor) which consisted in having his prostate gland massaged through the rectum. Finding this too expensive he confided in his roommate, who offered to do it for him if properly instructed. ¶ "That's simple. Here is how the doctor did it: First I bent way over, then he put his left hand on my back . . . say come to think of it he put both hands on my back."

·136·

Peggy, a young girl, was once asked whether she knew the difference between a spider and a fly. ¶ "Well, no," she admitted. "You see I never opened a spider."

·137·

A hen and a duck were passing the time of day and during the course of their conversation the duck asked the hen how much she was getting for her eggs. ¶ "Thirty five cents a dozen," replied the hen. "How much are you getting?" ¶ "I'm getting forty five cents," answered the duck. "But of course my eggs are much larger." ¶ "Huh," said the hen as she walked away, "I should stretch my ass for ten cents."

·138·

"I'd give five hundred dollars if I could fuck that one in the end in the first row." said one man to another as they were watching a big musical review. ¶ "Well Jack," said the other man. "I know the producer personally and I'll see if I can fix it up for you." ¶ Sure enough he fixed it up so that Jack was introduced to the girl after the show that night. ¶ "I'll stay with you from whatever time we go to bed tonight until seven tomorrow morning," said the girl, "if you pay me the five hundred in advance." ¶ He paid her the five hundred and took her to a cabaret, where, in his joyous mood of anticipation he became very drunk and when they arrived at her hotel, immediately passed out. ¶ When he awoke in the morning there was a note which read: "I carried out my end of the contract. Sorry you weren't able to fuck me." ¶ He went to the nearest butcher shop, borrowed the largest cleaver in the place, put his prick on the chopping block and aimed a blow. Having to pull his body back to strike he naturally missed his prick. He tried three times to no avail, then said, "You little son-of-a-bitch, you can miss a two foot cleaver, but you can't find your way into a five hundred dollar pussy."

·139·

Sammy had been boasting to his boss that he could fuck thirty times in a night. The boss was skeptical, however, and went up to Sam's room, where sure enough he fucked Liza thirty three times. ¶ The boss, being a Scotchman saw here a grand opportunity for making some money from his friends, and bet them all that Sam could fuck thirty times a night. The eventful night came and Sammy fucked eighteen, nineteen, twenty times. After the twenty fourth and fifth times, Sammy looked as though he could go no further and sure enough fainted just as he completed the twenty sixth fuck. ¶ The boss was furious and when Sam was revived said "What's the matter with you Sam? Didn't you tell me you could fuck thirty times without any trouble?" ¶ "Ah don't know what's the matter boss. This afternoon at the rehearsal everythin' went jus' fine and dandy."

·140·

An Englishman followed a girl up the winding steps of a Fifth Ave. bus. When they reached the top he thought it would be nice to start a conversation with the lady, and said, "Kind of 'airy, ain't it?" ¶ "Sure it is," she said. "What did you expect to see, ostrich feathers?"

·141·

Professor Albertstein was lecturing a body of students about the new and amazing discovery of the prehistoric animal, called the Wow. It was larger than any other animal and had some habits peculiar and different from any living thing discovered heretofore. ¶ After the lecture, the professor invited questions from the students and one chap asked, "Professor, why was this animal called the Wow by the people of that time?" ¶ "That question," answered the professor, "Occurred to the man who discovered the Wow and after much research and study, he found out that the Wow only shit once a year, but when he did WOW!"

·142·

Misha Gladcomofsky Venefuksky, had saved up enough money at last to make a trip to Moscow. He had never been in a big city before and was anxious to see how things were going since the revolution. His wife, Rosenshinska Filthakunska Shitzinbedka, bid him goodbye and told him to be careful of the city slickers. ¶ He arrived in Moscow safely but was amazed to see the starvation that was prevalent in such a big city. He had wandered around all day taking in the sights and about dusk had to take a terrible shit. He knew not where to go, but couldn't wait, so went into a hallway next to a butcher shop and proceeded to shit. ¶ Meanwhile, a Moscovite had entered the butcher shop, asked for a pound of meat and ran out of the store without paying for it. When Misha emerged from the hallway with the shit neatly tied up in his handkerchief, he was nabbed by the butcher who dragged him into the store, took the bag of shit and put it on the scales. As it only weighed three quarters of a pound, he beat Misha terribly and kicked him out. ¶ When Misha arrived home some days later, he was met at the door by his wife who asked, "Well, Misha Gladcomofsky Venefuksky, how did you like the big city? Is it nice there, do they get plenty to eat, are they happy and singing all the time? Come, tell Rosenshinska Filthakunska Shitzinbedka all about your trip." ¶ "Rosenshenska Likapricka," he addressed her by her pet name. "If you think we're bad off here having to eat dead rats and cats you're mistaken. We're very lucky, for in Moscow all the butchers sell is shit, and furthermore they beat you up if you don't shit at least a pound."

·143·

Q: Why do women have legs?
A: So they don't leave snail trails when they walk.

·144·

A doctor was questioning a male patient in an attempt
to find the reason for the latter's run-down condition.
The patient, a married man, said his domestic relations
were "all right." ¶ "But I mean," said the physician,
"how often do you have sexual relations with your wife?"
¶ "Oh, about three times a night, usually," was the
response. ¶ "Any girl friends?" pursued the doctor. ¶
"One," said the patient, "but I don't usually fuck her
more than a couple of times a day." ¶ "Any other
women?" asked the doc. ¶ "Well, my stenographer's a
pretty lively sort, and of course I have to slip it into her
now and then during the day." ¶ "Any others?" ¶ "Well,
you see, I'm in the cloak and suit business and I have to
keep the models feeling good. That means a few more
fucks." ¶ "Any others?" ¶ "Not many. Only when a
buyer comes to town I have to take him out for a little
time. Of course that means a bit of cunt." ¶ The doctor
was ready with his diagnosis. ¶ "There's nothing the
matter with you but too much fucking," he said. ¶ The
patient looked immensely relieved. ¶ "Are you sure?"
¶ "Absolutely." ¶ "Well, you don't know how you
relieve me, doctor. I was afraid it was masturbation."

·145·

George Wilkins, perambulating down the street one
evening, met Thomas Hunkins who was escorting two
ladies. ¶ "Evenin'," said George. "Where might you
be going?" ¶ "Oh," replied Thomas, "I'm takin' two
ladies to a ball. An' where might you be goin'?" ¶ "Vice
versa," said George.

·146·

Uncle George and Auntie Mabel
Fainted at the breakfast table
Children, let this be a warning
Never do it in the morning.

·147·

Little Jackie stuck his arm out of the train window, causing his father to pull him in and box his ears soundly. An old lady came over to the father and reprimanded him for striking his son, saying, "I'm going to make trouble for you." ¶ The father answered, "You see dat goil sittin' over dere wit de big belly? Dat's mine daughter, Sylvia, vat she's in de family vay vitout a husband. My vife she's dead in de baggage coch ahead. I just lost all my money in Vall street. Ikey here just shit in his pants and Izzy swallowed de tickets for de conductor, and you're going to make trouble for me?"

·148·

A fellow walked into a fish market and said, "How much are crabs today?" ¶ "Forty cents a dozen, sir." ¶ "Well," said the fellow, "Shake hands with a millionaire."

·149·

Before becoming respectable and marrying the General, she had had the reputation of being the towns most popular whore, who would take on any one regardless of size and as many as came in a night. ¶ One night the General was giving a swell party and among the guests was a fellow who had slept with her while she was in the profession. ¶ He recognized her and tried to make polite conversation, but she high-hatted him and walked away with her nose in the air. ¶ Not accustomed to being treated in this manner, he followed her and called her some very vile names. ¶ She ran excitedly in to the General who was playing chess and sobbing said, "Oh, my deah General, I've been insulted by a young whippersnapper and demand that you get me an apology." ¶ "There, there, my dear," said he, "Don't get excited. What did he call you?" ¶ "He called me an old whore and a cocksucker." ¶ "Well my dear, that is nothing to get peeved about. Why, I haven't been in the army for years and people still call me General."

·150·

The pastor had long been worrying about the dwindling congregations at the Sunday evening services. Finally he had a bright idea. ¶ "Next Sunday night," he announced, "we are going to discuss the topic: "What is the best part of a woman's body? Your pastor will ask yo' all to contribute your ideas." ¶ When next Sunday night arrived the church was jammed. Deacon Simpson started the symposium with a panegyric on woman's hair. Deacon Brown followed with an equally eloquent eulogy of woman's eyes. Brother White spoke no less enthusiastically of woman's mouth. The next speaker was Brother Johnson, who spoke long and feelingly on the beauties of a woman's breasts. As he concluded the pastor spied a hand waving frantically down toward the rear of the congregation. ¶ "Well, brudder Smith?" he said. ¶ Brother Smith got to his feet. ¶ "I move that this meetin' be adjourned," he shouted. "First thing you know some fool will be gettin' up and tellin' de truth!"

·151·

A Jewish carpenter put up a partition in a whore house and asked the madam for thirty dollars for the job. She replied that she hadn't thirty dollars, but that he was perfectly welcome to take it out in trade. ¶ "Can I take it out on you?" he asked the madam. ¶ "Sure," she said, flattered by the proposition. ¶ When she lay on the bed undressed, he stuck his thumb up her cunt and his index finger up her ass-hole and said, "Giff me the thirty dollars now, or I pull out the partition."

·152·

It had taken a long time, but by using all his arts and persuasion, he finally "laid" her. When it was over there was silence for a few minutes, then he asked: ¶ "Well, how did you like it?" ¶ "Oh, well enough," she replied, "but I can't say that I think much of your organ." ¶ "No?" he countered. "Well, I didn't expect to play in an auditorium."

·153·

A famous writer was being interviewed by reporters
at her home. ¶ "This is a very nice little place you have
here, Miss." said one. ¶ "Yes," she answered, "Just a
little place to lay my head, and my friends."

·154·

Mrs. Ginsberg, noticing that her stomach was becoming
rather swollen, went to the doctor, who asked her to send
him a specimen of her urine the following day. ¶ She
sent her son Bernard to the doctor's office the following
day with a tin can containing the urine. On the way Bernie
fell down and spilled the can of urine. He scooped as
much of it from the sidewalk as he could get and proceeded
to the doctor. ¶ "Vell, doctor," inquired Mrs. Ginsberg
when she returned a few days later, "Vat did you find?"
¶ "Mrs. Ginsberg," he answered, "I find that you are
going to give birth to a litter of pigs." ¶ "Oy, Oy," she
Oy, Oyed, "You can't even trust a weenie these days."

·155·

A young man from the South married a Yankee girl
and took her to the ancestral Virginia homestead for their
honeymoon. The old housekeeper who still presided in
the colonial home set about to see that the bridal couple
got a magnificent supper on the day of their arrival. But
they didn't come downstairs, and the dinner got cold.
The woman put it away, saying to herself that they should
have a fine breakfast the next morning, anyway. But they
didn't appear for breakfast. The same thing occurred at
noon, and she had to clear away the dinner she had cooked
and set out so temptingly. As supper-time was approaching,
Maizie was stacking up a pile of fragrantly steaming
griddle-cakes when the bride appeared. ¶ "Oh, Maizie,"
exclaimed the bride, looking at the cakes, "you know
what I like!" ¶ "Indeed I do, honey," responded Maizie,
"but you have to eat sometime."

·156·

A poor man, a Catholic, went to his priest to arrange for a mass for his wife who had recently died. The priest agreed. ¶ "But," he added, "you understand a mass costs money." ¶ "How much?" asked the bereaved husband. ¶ "A high mass is ten dollars," answered the priest, "and a low mass is five dollars." ¶ "But I haven't any money," the man pleaded. ¶ "Haven't you any relatives you could get the money from?" asked the priest. ¶ "No, none of my relatives have any money." ¶ "What relatives have you?" persisted the priest. ¶ "Only two unmarried sisters, who are both nuns." ¶ "Stop," said the priest, indignantly. "Don't let me hear you say your sisters are unmarried. They are brides of Christ." ¶ "Brides of Christ?" ¶ "Yes," said the priest, "brides of Christ." ¶ "Well then, Father, you go ahead and say the mass, and charge it to my brother-in-law."

·157·

A famous actress was arguing with George Bernard Shaw. ¶ "Women are much better bed-mates than men," said she. ¶ "I quite agree with you." said Shaw. "But women can't do nearly as many things as men can." ¶ "Balls!" answered she. ¶ "Don't you wish you had some?" retorted George.

·158·

A travelling salesman had been sending reports to his New York firm: "Didn't get an order from this big store, but had a long talk with the buyer and made a good connection. It's a feather in my cap." ¶ He had travelled all over the country, without getting an order but always ended the report by saying it was a feather in his cap. ¶ One day he received the following wire from the firm: "You had better take all those feathers, stick them up your ass and fly home. The firm is bankrupt and we can't send you carfare."

·159·

For months a handsome man sat every night in the first row of the Civic Repertory Theatre. Every night before and after the show the leading lady would receive flowers from the unknown gentleman accompanied by poetic notes telling her of her beauty and marvellous acting ability. ¶ One night he summoned up enough courage to go back stage and knock timidly on the famous actress's dressing room door. ¶ "Come in," commanded the deep husky voice. ¶ He entered, walked directly over to where she sat, fell on his knees at her feet, and said, "You are the most beautiful person in the world. I want you for my wife." ¶ "All right," she answered, "Bring her around. Maybe I can use her."

·160·

While dusting the statuary in a sculptors studio, the maid accidentally knocked over one of the male figures, breaking off the prick. She quickly pasted it back on, but when the sculptor returned he immediately noticed what had happened. ¶ "How did you notice it?" asked the maid. ¶ "I had it hanging down and you made it stick up," he replied. ¶ That's the only way I ever saw them," said the maid.

·161·

A messenger boy had delivered some flowers to Marlene Anderson's dressing room and took the opportunity to tell her how beautiful he thought she was. ¶ "Thank you," said Marlene, "But run along now, I must get undressed." ¶ She proceeded to undress and after some time she turned around to find the boy still in the room, staring at her. ¶ She handed him a quarter and said, "Run along now little boy." ¶ When she was completely nude, she turned around to find the little fellow still there. "You had better run along now, I hear somebody coming." ¶ "Miss Anderson," he replied, "You have marvellous hearing. That's me."

·162·

An old man, plodding feebly along the street, met a little girl who was crying bitterly. ¶ "What's the matter, little girl?" he asked. ¶ Still sobbing, the girl replied: ¶ "I want one of those things like my brother's got, that sticks out and lies down and sticks out again!" ¶ The old man began to cry too.

·163·

On a dark rainy night the door of a midtown hotel opened with a bang and a gargantuan male figure strode up to the desk clerk and demanded in a hoarse voice. "I gotta have a room." The clerk informed him, that the hotel was crowded and this would be an impossibility. The ire of the man overcame him and, pounding his fist on the desk, breaking a piece off, he cried in a heated voice, "I gotta have a room." The clerk was frightened and finally appeased the man by remembering a double room that was half occupied. He requested the tenant to permit the renting of half the room, to which the latter acquiesced, and the ponderous visitor was thus accommodated. ¶ The bed, now doing double service, remained quiet for a while, until a grunting from one of the occupants disturbed it, and a bated breath murmured, "Turn over." The bed shook, with the execution of this movement. "Take down your pajamas," came the next command. Then the huge shadow of the intruder could be seen on the wall, with a mighty ten inch joy prong outlined on the wall, as stiff as the mustache on a Tasmanian wombat. This huge instrument disappeared a quarter of the way into the distended rectum of the unfortunate bed companion, and a question was asked, "Is that all right?" ¶ The quavering answer came back, "I guess-s so." A thrust, and one half had disappeared. ¶ "How's that? O.K.?" ¶ To which a drawn out wail, answered, "I guess-s-s so." ¶ A huge push, a startled shriek, and the triumphant question, "I guess that's O.K. now?" ¶ The answer came in gurgling response, "I ghec gho."

·164·

Lady Smith was taking a golf lesson from the pro at St. Andrews, Scotland. She took a stance and he said to her, "Ay, my lady, ye'll get nowhere, standing like that. Ye must put your feet furrther aparrt." ¶ Lady Smith moved her feet apart. Jock shook his head and said sadly, "That'll never do in the worrld. Put them furrther aparrt." ¶ A second time she did. Again he shook his head— "Lady Smith, Lady Smith, will ye listen to me? Put your feet furrther aparrt! Ye'll never hit a ball in the worrld like that." ¶ Lady Smith looked at him and said, "Jock, Jock you men are all alike."

·165·

"What are those funny looking things you've got strung around the wall?" asked the fairy as he entered the doctor's office. ¶ "Those are petrified cunts. My hobby is collecting them and what you see here is the result of much searching and expense on my part," answered the physician. ¶ The fairy then went to each petrified cunt, wet his finger, rubbed it on each specimen and put it to his lips. After doing this to the entire collection, he turned to the doctor and said, "I'm sorry to tell you you've been cheated. Someone included two ass holes on you."

·166·

A travelling salesman riding through the south, picked up a young woman on the train. On propositioning her, he found that she was unwell, but when she retired that night, he crept into her berth anyway. ¶ He woke with a start the following morning, dressed hurriedly, ran to the platform and inquired of a young porter: "What station is this?" ¶ "Birmingham, sir, who hit you in the mouth?" answered the boy.

·167·

"Mornin', Zenobia." ¶ "Morning William." ¶ "Where you going?" ¶ "I'm going to get bread." ¶ "Bred to who?"

·168·

A cowboy had just been married and was spending the first night with his wife at a small hotel. She noticed that as he removed each of his garments, he very carefully put them on a shelf in the closet. Hat, spurs, boots and everything else were tucked snugly on the shelf and the door carefully locked. His wife was led to inquire the meaning of these strange actions, to which Will replied, "Wall, I ain't never fucked a woman before, but if they're anything like cows this room will be overflowing with shit in no time."

·169·

A man anxious for a little love accosted a lady in the street who apparently was not adverse to lending herself to his purposes, except that he did not have sufficient funds to pay her regular fee. However a bargain was struck whereby he might handle the lady's recesses for the 25 cents his budget provided for such necessities. ¶ They found an unfrequented alley where, after the lady had lifted her skirts, the light was so dim that he was forced to ask her permission to make use of his pocket lighter for purpose of illumination. She assented graciously and our hero, holding the lighter close, was astounded at the sight which confronted him. Long lustrous waves of luxuriant hair covered the sacred mount. He could not refrain from expressing his admiration. ¶ The lady was flattered at the tribute and added that many had rewarded and praised that hirsute adornment. ¶ "But it is magnificent," cried the man. "So thick, so impenetrable. Would you mind if I asked you a very personal question?" ¶ "Not at all," said the lady. ¶ "Well then," said the man, "is it possible for you to urinate through that?" ¶ "Oh yes indeed," said the lady. ¶ "Then I suggest that you begin at once," said our hero, "because you're on fire."

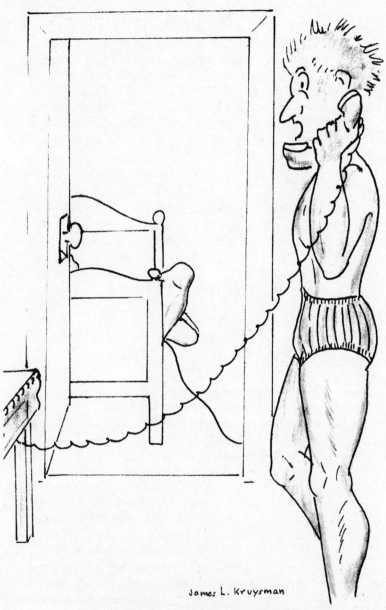

James L. Kruysman

"I've been replaced in the office by a computer, and
in the bedroom by a vibrator!"

·170·

Simple Gracie decided to take out some insurance. The company doctor called for the examination. ¶ "Gracie, when were you sick last?" ¶ "Oh, Oh, Doctor the twenty sixth of last month." ¶ "No Gracie, you don't understand. When were you in the hospital last?" ¶ "Oh, about three months ago to see my brother." ¶ "No Gracie. When were you bed-ridden last." ¶ "Oh Doctor, last night and it was wonderful."

·171·

"Mrs. Blatz," said that lady's friend and neighbor, "I know you're a widow and it's none of my business, but people are talking. You're a middle-aged woman, and when a 17-year-old boy calls on you every night and stays late, it looks funny." ¶ "You should know it's purely platonic," Mrs. Blatz replied. ¶ "What do you mean— platonic, an' him leavin' sometimes at 2 o'clock in the mornin'?" ¶ "Platonic I said an' platonic I mean," repeated Mrs. Blatz. "It's play for him an' it's a tonic for me."

·172·

"Have you seen the new school marm yet?" inquired Josh of Zeke while the boys were sitting and spitting into the fire at the general store. ¶ "Yes, I had her out the other day." ¶ "You didn't." ¶ "Yes I did." ¶ "What did you do?" ¶ "Wall, I got old Dobbin hitched up to the buggy and me and the schoolmarm we rode up the road a piece and I stopped Dobbin and put my hand right on her ankle." ¶ "You didn't." ¶ "Yes I did." ¶ "What did you do then?" ¶ "Wall, we rode up the road another little piece and I put my hand right on her knee." ¶ "You didn't." ¶ "Yes I did." ¶ "What did you do then?" ¶ "Wall, we rode up the road another little piece and I put my hand right on it." ¶ "You didn't." ¶ "Yes I did." ¶ "What did it feel like?" ¶ "Don't know, I had me mittens on."

·173·

Bill was walking to work one morning when he met a friend. ¶ "Morning, Bill," said the friend. "Did you know your pants are unbuttoned." ¶ "Sure," said Bill, and walked on. ¶ A little farther along he met another friend. ¶ "Hey, Bill," said the latter, "your pants are unbuttoned." ¶ "Sure, I know it," replied Bill. ¶ "Well, what's the matter with you?" demanded the friend. "Why don't you button them up?" ¶ "Because I'm experimenting," Bill replied. ¶ "What do you mean, experimenting?" ¶ "Well, you see, it's this way," Bill explained. "Yesterday morning I walked out with my collar unbuttoned, and I got a stiff neck."

·174·

A Boston socialite was a little ashamed of the grammatical lapses of his wife, newly acquired from the follies. He sent her to England for a year to round off the angles of her style and diction. ¶ On the day of her return he watched with eagerness as the boat slipped alongside the pier. There she was waving frantically to him and shouting. "Hello darling have you been blue while I was gone?" ¶ "Blown, dear, blown!" shouted back the Bostonian.

·175·

Gertie was about to be married. The day before the wedding, Belle, who worked in the same office, took her to lunch. ¶ "Listen," said Belle, "I'm married, myself, and I'd like to give you a tip. If you want to have a swell wedding night, see that your husband eats a lot of raw oysters for supper." ¶ Gertie, a little bashful but grateful for the hint, said she would. ¶ When she returned from her honeymoon trip the two girls again went to lunch together. ¶ "Well, Gert," said Belle, "how was it?" ¶ "First-rate," said Gertie. "Fine." ¶ "Did you do what I told you to?" ¶ "Yes," said Gertie, "but, somehow, it turned out a little odd. I fed him a dozen raw oysters for supper that night, like you said. But, do you know, only eight of them worked!"

·176·

"Dot buyer from that big store and me is like this," said Cohen crossing his fingers. "Venever he comes to town he von't see nobody bat me. Ve haff dinner togedder, go to shows togedder and a cabaret later togedder. In fect, den ve go to a hotel und sleep togedder. Only he has one verry funny habeet. Ven ve go to bed togedder he alvays takes my head and pushes it to de meedle off de bed." ¶ "Vat do you do den, Cohen?" ¶ "Vat can I do? He's my best costomer."

·177·

An AC/DC actress died and of course went to heaven. She knocked on the door and when St. Peter opened it she said. "I'm the famous Miss G. and I want to get in." ¶ "Just a minute," St. Peter said and closing the door disappeared. ¶ She waited for about ten minutes and then impatient she knocked on the door again. "Say," she said, "I'm the famous Miss G. and I want to get in." ¶ "Just a minute," St. Peter said, and disappeared. ¶ She waited another ten minutes and then she got mad. She kicked on the door and shouted and cursed. When St. Peter opened the door she said, "Say what's the idea? I'm Miss G. I'm a well known actress from New York and I want to get in. "What's the idea?" ¶ "Yes, yes," St. Peter said soothingly. "We were just finding a suitable hiding place for the virgin Mary."

·178·

Another actress gave a costume party, all the guests appearing as popular songs. The first guest to appear was a beautiful nude girl with a bunch of multi-colored ribbons hanging from her throat. ¶ "And what may you represent?" said Miss Pickwick. ¶ "There's a Rainbow O'er My Shoulder," said the girl. ¶ The next guest was a nude man arrayed in a grass skirt. ¶ "And what may you represent?" "Turkey in the Straw," said the man. "But if you don't get that naked woman out of the way I'll be 'Comin' Thru the Rye.' "

·179·

A young accountant took his gay wife to a house party, given by the office manager. In the course of the evening the manager and his wife got very drunk several times and disappeared out into the night, only to return perfectly sober. Flattered as he was by the attentions his superior was paying his wife, the situation was becoming more than he could bear with equanimity. ¶ The next time they went out, he waited for a few minutes, and then followed the pair into the garden. He found his wife sitting alone on the grass and asked her what she was doing there. ¶ "I'm just taking a piss, darling." ¶ He took his index and middle fingers, stuck them up her cunt, held his fingers to the light of the house, spread them apart and said, "Piss don't make windows."

·180·

For some time a young man had been expecting his wife to give birth to a baby, and one morning he telephoned the office that he wouldn't be there that day. His wife's labor pains had begun. The next day he appeared. ¶ "What is it—a boy or a girl?" asked his fellow-workers. ¶ He thought a moment and replied: ¶ "It was a bicycle." ¶ The others put their heads together. Plainly the strain had done something to him. One of them approached him again. ¶ "What did your wife have?" he asked. ¶ This time he cogitated longer but finally replied: ¶ "It was a motorcycle." ¶ They went to the boss and told him about it. The boss called Henry in. ¶ "What was it your wife had?" he asked kindly. Henry thought hard, scratched his head, and answered: ¶ "An automobile." ¶ "You're kind of worn out," said the boss. "Better go home and get some rest. ¶ When Henry got home he walked at once into the bedroom. ¶ "Say," he demanded, as his wife looked up from the bed. "What was it you had?" ¶ "A miscarriage," she replied. ¶ "Gosh," he said, "I knew it was something on wheels."

·181·

Mr. Goldberg, whose wife had a prodigiously spacious cunt, took her to the doctor to see if the defect could be remedied. The doctor, an amateur in plastic surgery, grafted one of the good woman's ears to her lower orifice, and the operation was entirely successful. ¶ A few weeks later he met his patient and in a professional manner inquired, "How do you feel Mrs. Goldberg, have you any pain?" ¶ Mrs. Goldberg lifted her skirts, raised her leg and answered, "Vill you please talk a liddle louder, doctor?"

·182·

Mrs. O'Leary's husband had been dead a year, but his widow never ceased, whenever she had opportunity to talk to the parish priest, to extol the virtues and mourn the passing of the late lamented. The priest, ordinarily a patient man—and remembering that during the lifetime of the deceased Mrs. O'Leary made him pretty miserable with her vixenish temper—decided he would hear no more. The next time the widow started her eulogy of O'Leary, he listened quietly until she said: ¶ "And, Father, he was so kind, so gentle! He never beat me. He never touched a hair of me. Never a hair—" ¶ "What marksmanship!" interrupted the priest, dryly.

·183·

A new bellboy was being instructed in the elements of his job. ¶ "Courtesy and tact," said the bellhop captain, in conclusion, "courtesy and tact! Them's the things to remember." ¶ A few days later the new boy was sent to a room with icewater. When he returned he reported to his boss as follows: ¶ "I knocked on the door but I didn't get any answer, so I went right in. The bathroom door was open and a swell dame was getting into the tub, all naked. But I remembered what you said about courtesy. So I said 'Excuse me.' Then I remembered about tact, so I said 'Excuse me, SIR.' I guess that 'sir' was tact, eh?"

·184·

Little Junior wasn't much help while the bridge game was in progress. His mother tried desperately to get him to leave the room but Junior was having more fun reading off the cards in the hands of those playing, romping back and forth, and playing fire-engine. His mother was distracted. Suddenly one of the players, a gray haired man, suggested that she let him try his efforts on the boy. He led Junior out and for the rest of the afternoon, there was no sight nor sound of him. His mother was very grateful to the gentleman who had so successfully established peace for a few hours and asked him whether he wouldn't be kind enough to tell her what he had done. ¶ "Why certainly," replied the gentleman. "I taught him how to masturbate!"

·185·

A famous movie star, the particular intimate of a noted director, gave a big party to celebrate the completion of a new film. The director refused to drink anything, as he had to start work on a new picture the next day. Amid the gaiety the star filled her slipper with champagne, rubbed some of the fluid on her arms, then some on her breasts and lastly a generous amount on her twotch. ¶ Next morning a production official, waiting on the set for the director to appear, angrily wanted to know why he hadn't shown up. ¶ "To tell the truth he's got a fearful hangover," confided the assistant director.

·186·

Mr. Reginald Smithervilt went to the barber shop to get his usual morning shave. ¶ "Why, Mr. Smithervilt," said the barber, "You have a blonde curly hair in your mustache." ¶ "Very likely." said Smithervilt. "I always kiss my wife on the head when I go to work." ¶ "You will excuse me Mr. Smithervilt," said the barber, "But you have shit all over your neck-tie."

·187·

Patrick O'Murphy was dead. He went up to heaven and was met by St. Peter, who said, "Hullo Pat, me boy, I'm glad to see you here. But I have some very sad news to break to you. Pat, there ain't a place left in this old heaven. We're full to the brim with people like O'Meara, Kelly, your own father and mother and many others, all good Catholics like yourself. You really belong here Pat, but since there ain't no room you'll have to go down to the devil." ¶ So Pat went down to the devil, who met him at the gates of hell. ¶ "Hullo Pat," said he, "Sure and I'm glad to see you down here." ¶ "Hullo, yourself," said Pat. "Have you a place for me? St. Peter himself is just after telling me that heaven is filled up to capacity." ¶ "Sure Pat, I'm pretty overcrowded myself down here. But I just have two places left and you can have whichever one of them you want." ¶ "What are the two places?" asked Pat, as they walked through the gates into hell. ¶ "One place is right over there in that red hot furnace and the other place is right over here in this barrel of shit up to your chin." ¶ Just then Pat heard a faint voice coming from the direction of the barrel. It was his old friend Mike, who sure enough was up to his lower lip in shit. ¶ "Hullo Pat," greeted Mike, are you coming in here with me?" He was holding his head as high as possible to keep from getting shit in his mouth. ¶ "Yes Mike, I think I'd rather go in there with you than go into that red hot furnace." ¶ "Well for Christ's sake, Pat, be careful not to make any waves when you come in."

·188·

An up-to-date boy was feeling an up-to-date girl, and as he stuck his finger up her cunt he said, "What, no cellophane?"

·189·

What three public institutions does a woman resemble? ¶ A dairy, a naval base, and a home for little children.

·190·

A pansy ran excitedly up to the cop on the beat and lisped, ¶ "Officer, I've been robbed." ¶ "You mean you've been fucked," retorted the cop. ¶ "I've been robbed too," said the fairy.

·191·

A gentleman came home unexpectedly one day to find his young wife clutching the erect penises of two of his friends, a third was screwing her from the rear while she was running her mouth up and down the organ of a fourth man who was lying supine before her. ¶ "Oh Mary, how can you, how can you?" cried the grief-stricken husband. ¶ "I've always been something of a flirt," she answered.

·192·

A fellow had been in an automobile accident and his lip was severely injured. A nurse offered her services to the doctor in case any blood or skin was needed for the poor fellow. ¶ It was necessary to take some skin from her cunt and graft it onto the fellow's lip, to save his face from disfigurement. ¶ The doctor met him about a year later and inquired, "How is your lip young fellow, since we grafted the nurse's skin on it?" ¶ "It's alright, doc, but every time I take a piss my lip quivers."

·193·

Marie was accustomed to having Tom stop by each day at lunch time. This day it was approaching one o'clock and no Tom. Marie was getting a very itchy feeling in her cunt. ¶ One o'clock passed and no Tom. Marie couldn't stand it any longer. She hitched up the horse and buggy and started hell bent down Main street to find Tom. The tail board of the buggy dropped off. A teen-ager standing in the street saw it and hollered, "Hey Marie don't you want your tail board?" ¶ Marie turned and yelled, "Hop on here you mind-reading fucker!"

·194·

A witty writer complained to her doctor that she could no longer get a man to satisfy her. "How," she asked. "Can I tell the length of a man's prick by outward appearances?" ¶ "The only way to tell is by the size of his feet. The bigger the feet, the bigger the meat." The doctor informed her. ¶ She cruised around in a taxicab that afternoon until she saw, standing in front of an employment agency, a young fellow wearing tremendous shoes. She picked him up, wined and dined him, and took him to her ducky little apartment. ¶ When he awoke the following morning, the lady had already left, but there was a five dollar bill on a table next to the bed accompanied by a note which read: "Take this five dollars with my compliments, and go out and buy yourself a pair of shoes that fit you."

·195·

The patient complained of chronic constipation, and the doctor gave him a supply of suppositories, directing him to use one every night when he went to bed. ¶ "If they don't bring you relief," said the physician, "come back in a week." ¶ In a week the patient was back, declaring his constipation was as bad as ever. ¶ "Did you use the suppositories?" asked the doctor. ¶ "Of course I did," responded the patient. "What the hell do you think I did—stick them up my ass?"

·196·

When an actress first came to Hollywood from Europe, she was fascinated by a cigarette holder that a fellow on the movie lot was using. She inquired about this strange device she had never seen before. ¶ After her days work, she went to a drug store and asked the clerk for one of those round rubber things that men use, which cost fifty cents. ¶ "What size do you wish, madam?" asked the clerk. "Giff me one that will fit a Camel." was the lady's answer.

·197·

A young married couple, with modern ideas, decided they would bring up their young son sensibly. So when he began to ask questions about sex they didn't tell him about the stork. They didn't even tell him about flowers and the pollen. They told him the facts, quite matter-of-factly. He was satisfied, and they felt very pleased, especially as he continued to be a normal, healthy, well-behaved youngster. One day, when he was 9 years old, he burst into the kitchen where his mother was getting dinner. ¶ "Mum," he exclaimed, "I had my first piece of tail today!" ¶ "What!" demanded the nonplussed mother. ¶ "I said I had my first piece of tail today." ¶ The mother called his father into the kitchen, and, turning to the boy, commanded: ¶ "Tell your father what you just told me." ¶ Addressing his father, the lad repeated: "I had my first piece of tail today." ¶ The father cast his eyes about the room until he espied a frying pan hanging on the wall. He reached to get it, when the wife exclaimed: ¶ "Oh, Henry, Henry, don't strike him with that!" ¶ "Strike him?" repeated the father. "I'm not going to strike him. I'm going to fry him an egg. You can't start out that way on cereals!"

·198·

It was during the height—or the depth—of the depression, that a man walked along Broadway shouting enthusiastically: ¶ "Oh, boy! Oh, boy! Oh, boy!" ¶ Finally an acquaintance stepped up to him. ¶ "Why all the 'Oh boys'?" asked the latter. ¶ "I was just thinking," the man replied, "if all the men were as hard as times are, and all the women as tight as money is—Oh, boy! Oh, boy! Oh, boy!"

·199·

A girl from an Ivy League college asked another if she had ever been psycho-analyzed. ¶ "No," the other replied, "but I've been ultra-violated."

·200·

Sam's wife had a peculiarity. She was much averse to wearing panties, or drawers of any sort. Sam couldn't persuade her to, and somehow he didn't like the idea of his wife going around thus unprotected. So one morning when Mrs. Sam awoke with a severe cold, he had an idea. When he got to his office he called up the family physician and asked him to call around to see Mrs. Sam. ¶ "And, doc," he said, "I want you to do something for me. My wife simply won't wear panties or bloomers or anything. If you can make her believe that's the reason she caught cold, I'll double your fee." ¶ In due time the doctor called to see Mrs. Sam. He examined her throat very carefully. ¶ "Mrs. Sam," he said, "I'll give you something for this cold—but if you want to avoid colds in the future you'll have to wear bloomers. It's evident that you don't." ¶ "Do you mean to say," demanded Mrs. Sam, "that you can look down my throat and see that I don't wear pants?" ¶ "Exactly," said the doctor. ¶ "Then," said Mrs. Sam, "doctor, will you kindly look up my ass-hole and tell me if my hat is on straight?"

·201·

A New York firm of mattress manufacturers for some time, at intervals of a year or so, received orders for several thousand mattresses to be sent to the interior of Africa. Finally the company's sales manager could no longer contain his curiosity as to what anybody could want with so many mattresses in the African jungles, and he wrote asking the African customer about it. In due time the reply came. It read: ¶ "Your query of recent date at hand. It's none of your damn business what we use the mattresses for, but if you must know, we use them as sanitary napkins for the elephants."

·202·

"Mary, do you know the difference between a salesman and a truck?" ¶ "No, I've never been under a truck."

·203·

The fat men have adopted a famous slogan. When they want a peep at their penis they croon ''Why don'cha come up and see me sometime.''

·204·

A farmer went to the city for a spell and left his wife and the hired man in charge of the farm. As he returned home he was met on the road by the hired man. ¶ ''Sy,'' said the hired man, ''I have some awful bad news for you. Those twenty seven new cows of yours have been stolen.'' ¶ ''What other news?'' asked Sy. ¶ ''The new barn burned down and all your horses have hoof and mouth disease.'' ¶ ''Any other news?'' ¶ ''Yes, the rain ruined the entire crop.'' ¶ ''Haven't you got any good news for me at all?'' asked Sy. ¶ ''Oh yes, you know those bleeding spells your wife had in her cunt? Well I've got them stopped.''

·205·

Pat went to see a doctor. ''Doctor,'' said he. ''I'm a hard workin' man alayin' thim bricks all day and then not bein' able to shit for over a week now. Can't you give me somethin' tha' would make me shit?'' ¶ ''Sure Pat, I'll fix you up. Take two of these pills tonight, they'll make you shit alright.'' ¶ Pat went home and to make sure took four instead of the advised two pills. He came back the following day and said, ''Doctor thim pills you give me didn't work. Give me somethin' that'll *surely* make me shit.'' ¶ The doctor prescribed something much more potent but Pat came back the next day with the same story. This time he was given a physic that is used only on horses. And still it didn't work. ¶ ''Let me have a look at your ass-hole Pat?'' asked the doctor at this time. After the examination he exclaimed, ''Why man no wonder you couldn't shit. Your ass-hole is all stopped up with cement.'' ¶ ''Shure, and I remember now,'' said Pat. ''The last time I shit on the job, I wiped me ass with one of thim there cement bags.''

·206·

A northern gentleman went down south to visit a southern gentleman. Nothing in the southern colonel's mansion was too good for him. "Southern hospitality," said his host, "is what we're noted for, and I want to prove to you that we live up to our reputation." ¶ "What, I wonder, would the colonel think of me, after treating me so wonderfully, if he were to find me screwing his daughter out here in the cotton?" thought the city gentleman. ¶ Just then the colonel came along and after looking down at the pair for some time said to his daughter, "Darling, what did I teach you about hospitality? Lift your ass higher; the gentleman's balls are dragging in the mud."

·207·

A motorcycle cop finally overtook a speeding automobile. ¶ "Draw up there," he said sternly to the fair and flushed young woman at the wheel. "You were going 70 miles an hour." ¶ "Sure I was. What of it?" she retorted. ¶ The cop stared at her. ¶ "Ain't you the fresh egg?" he finally got out. "I ought to be," she answered. "I was just laid an hour ago."

·208·

The children had just returned to school after their summer vacation. The teacher was asking them what they had done and seen during this time. She came to little Johnnie, and asked, "Well, Johnnie, where did you go for your vacation?" ¶ "Went to me uncle's farm." ¶ "Did you see anything of interest there?" ¶ "Naw, nothin." ¶ "Well, didn't you do anything interesting while at the farm?" ¶ "Naw, nothin." ¶ "Come now Johnnie, you must have seen something or done something all the time you were away. Didn't you see a cow or a pig or a chicken?" ¶ "Yes teacher, I saw a chicken, and Jesus Christ teacher she laid an egg this big, teacher, honestly this big." ¶ "What did you say, Johnnie?" asked the teacher horrified. ¶ "I said goodbye asshole."

·209·

Mr. John Miller walked into his physician's office one afternoon, and taking out his prick said, "Doctor, cut two inches off here right away." ¶ The doctor was puzzled, but did not wish to argue with Miller, who was one of his best customers, and did as he was bid. ¶ When he had cut the two inches off, Miller said, "Now cut another inch off." ¶ The doctor protested to no avail, so he cut another inch from the prick of Mr. Miller. ¶ "Now doc," said Miller, "Sew the first two inches back on." ¶ The doctor did as he was ordered, and when he had finished asked, "What's the idea Mr. Miller, of all this cutting off and sewing on?" ¶ "I wanted to get rid of that one inch in the middle because that's the part that always bent."

·210·

A beautiful prostitute accosted a switchman in the rail-road yards. The switchman wasn't particularly interested in fucking the woman, but he had a sudden idea about amusing himself at her expense. It was dark, and he led her behind a freight car, laid her down, picked up a coupling pin, and inserted it in her. He gave it a few vigorous pushes and then lay still, waiting for her comments. There were none, and after a few minutes he asked: ¶ "Like it?" ¶ "Lordy," she responded, "I sure am glad you said somethin'. Your tool's so cold I was afraid you were dead!"

·211·

A woman, testifying against a man from her own block whom she had accused of rape, told the court she was leaning over the rail of her porch when the defendant approached her from the rear, lifted her skirts, inserted his penis, and pushed it in—all the way. ¶ "What did you do?" asked the court. ¶ "Why, judge," she replied, "I pushed right back. I'm not goin' to let no neighbor push me off my own front porch!"

·212·

Harold was quite an inventor. He applied at the local bank for a loan of ten thousand dollars, which he promised to turn into a million. The invention he hoped to market was one which made a woman's pussy taste like an orange. The cautious banker, turned the proposition down. ¶ A year later the banker in going through his accounts, came across a depositor with a million and a half dollars to his credit. Upon investigation he recognized the man with the orange patent as the depositor. ¶ He invited Harold to his office, and after congratulating him on his great success, remarked, "I wish I had seen the possibilities in that invention of yours." ¶ "I couldn't sell that idea any place, so I changed it. I perfected an orange which tastes like a pussy."

·213·

A young porter got married one afternoon and came back to work the next morning. His boss asked him how he liked being married. ¶ "Alright, boss, but that woman sure is mighty funny." ¶ "How come George?" ¶ "Well you see, boss, it's like this; I was kinda tired last night and I went to bed about nine o'clock. Along about eleven o'clock my woman said to me, 'Well how about it?' ¶ "I didn't pay no attention to her. Twelve o'clock she said to me again 'Well, George, how about it?' ¶ "I didn't know what the woman meant and I didn't pay no attention." ¶ "Long about two o'clock, she said to me; 'Well, honey, how about it?' ¶ "Then I got kinda mad, and I said to her, how about what?" ¶ "She said to me, 'How about gettin off me an lettin me take a piss?' "

·214·

One day when the store was out of boy candies, she asked for a male chocolate bar. ¶ "What do you mean a male chocolate bar?" asked the clerk. ¶ "One with nuts," was the answer.

·215·

One famous author was sitting next to another writer at a dinner recently. In his usual facetious vein, Frank rose, and putting his hand on Mark's gleaming, hairless, dome said, "Say you know Mark, this feels just like my wife's ass." ¶ Mark ran his hand over his own head and said, "By God, Frank, so it does."

·216·

An American travelling in Europe visited an international whore house. He selected a very attractive dark skinned gal but when informed that the price for her was five dollars, changed his selection to a Chinese woman who cost but three. After an interval of several years he again visited this same house and was greeted by his Chinese lady who presented to him a young lad as his son. The usual courtesies having been exchanged the boy asked, "Say Dad, why is your skin so white and mine so yellow?" The American replied, "You little bastard, if I had had two more bucks at the time you would have been black."

·217·

During the war, with her husband at the front, Mrs. Jones was lonely enough to call upon Bridget, her servant, as companion and counselor as well as domestic. ¶ One day a laconic cablegram came from Tommy. "I got my D.S.O." ¶ "Now what can that mean?" she asked Bridget, and the two women puzzled over it for a while. ¶ "Heaven preserve ye!" said Bridget suddenly, "faith and I think he means, 'I got my Dick Shot Off.' " They decided that that might be it. ¶ The next day Mrs. Jones accosted Bridget with a letter in her hand. ¶ "I'm afraid you're right, Bridget," she said. "Here's his letter. I asked him for money and he says 'Go fuck yourself.' "

·218·

It was dusk, and the three men who sat by the hotel window could look across the alley into the opposite apartment without being seen. Their own room was dark, and they were talking of this and that, smoking and talking of many matters. Suddenly one of them nudged the others. ¶ "Shh!" he whispered. "Look there, across the alley." ¶ They looked. They saw a dim light in the room. At the window, in a chair, with his feet propped up on the sill, sat a man dressed simply in a bathrobe. He was smoking a cigar, puffing gently. Suddenly a woman came into sight, a young girl, well developed and wearing only a kimono. She walked around the room several times, finally came to a stop by the man's side. Deliberately she made him remove his feet from the sill and the cigar from his mouth. Then she sat down on his lap and began to kiss him and slip her hand under his robe. This went on for a few minutes and then they both rose, walked to the bed, took off their robes and indulged in a half-hour of sport with each other in full view of the silent watchers. ¶ Well-satisfied with their possessions of each other, they got out of bed. The woman disappeared into a side room and the man very calmly put on his bathrobe, sat down on the chair by the window, propped his feet on the sill and lit a cigar. Perhaps twenty minutes later she came in sight again, wearing the same kimono. She walked around the room several times, finally came to a stop beside the man. Deliberately she made him remove his feet from the sill and the cigar from his mouth. ¶ Just as she was about to sit down on his lap, one of the watchers across the alley cried: ¶ "Let's go, boys. This is where we came in before!"

·219·

Question: What is the position "68?"
Answer: You do me, and I'll owe you.

·220·

Mrs. Broadwaist of the Back Bay Broadwaists was giving a Shakespearean costume party for her swanky friends. The Fitzroys and Gotgelts came as Macbeth and Portia and Hamlet and King Lear. Imagine the surprise of the gathered guests when three young men entered the house and, throwing off their cloaks, revealed themselves dressed simply in bathing suits! ¶ Haughty monocles and lorgnettes stared at them in amazement. "Where in Shakespeare does one find bathing suits mentioned?" was whispered around the room. No one seemed to know the answer. ¶ Finally the guests lined up to be judged. The three young men stood on line too, all together. Just before the judges walked by them they took out small cardboard signs. Each of the young men pinned one of them over his chest on his bathing suit. From left to right, the signs read: "Hard"—"Wet"—"Soft". ¶ After lengthy deliberation the judges went into a huddle and then announced that the three young men in bathing suits were awarded first place in the Shakespearean costume contest. ¶ A little outraged, since her guests had gone to so much trouble, that so seemingly stupid a decision had been made, Mrs. Broadwaist demanded an explanation. ¶ "We believe we have judged rightly," was the reply. You see, "Hard" stands for "As You Like It"—"Wet" for "Midsummer's Night Dream" and "Soft" for "Twelfth Night."

·221·

This is the inside story of the execution of Mata Hari, beautiful female spy. ¶ She appeared before the firing squad clad only in a luxurious sable coat. Just before the men were given the order to fire, she gracefully dropped the coat from her shoulders, revealing a magnificent body. ¶ "Fire!" ordered the captain. ¶ None of the men obeyed, but Mata Hari fell dead. ¶ You wonder how she was killed? By flying buttons.

·222·

A young man, who intended to seduce a beautiful girl of whom he had been long enamoured, finally persuaded her to take a walk in the park with him one gentle spring evening. She was, he understood, an innocent soul and a "good" girl. Therefore he was amazed and physically unprepared for the act when they came to a secluded grotto and she hurriedly divested herself of all her clothes and stretched herself out on the cool grass. ¶ For some reason, he was carrying an umbrella. Not having had an erection as yet, he inserted the tip of his umbrella in the receptacle planned by nature to receive the male organ. She closed her eyes and sighed with pleasure. He pushed it deeper and deeper and she continued to moan in ecstasy. Finally he had buried the entire umbrella and his arm up to his shoulder in her cunt. ¶ "More! More!" she pleaded. ¶ The young man suddenly broke into a storm of oaths. ¶ "Why, you little bitch!" he exclaimed. "I didn't know you were so goddam horny! Do you realize the whole umbrella and my arm are in you now? What more do you expect me to do?" ¶ She writhed and moaned and finally gasped out: ¶ "Open the umbrella! Open the umbrella!"

·223·

A country girl had married a Broadway playboy. "Darling," she said, when they were about to go to bed for the first time, "I don't know anything about this business, so you'll have to show me what to do." ¶ Thinking this would be a good chance to break her in right, he made her suck his cock. ¶ The next day she went to visit her mother and in the course of the conversation, burst out crying as though her heart would break. "What is the matter, dear?" asked the mother. ¶ "Oh mother, I so wanted to have children and now I know I just never shall have them," she sobbed. ¶ "Why?" inquired the mother. ¶ "Because I am sure I shall never learn to swallow that dreadful stuff."

·224·

A rather scared-looking, delicate young man was brought into court to testify that he had witnessed a young couple indulging in sexual intercourse behind some bushes in a public park. Put on the stand, he took the oath and waited nervously for the judge to question him. ¶ "What is your occupation?" demanded the jurist. ¶ The young man trembled. "I'm a poet, Your Honor," he said, fidgeting. ¶ "Did you see this man and woman in the park?" ¶ "Yes, sir." ¶ "And what were they doing?" the judge asked. ¶ "Fucking," the poet replied. ¶ The judge went white with rage. A titter ran through the courtroom at the witness's naivete. ¶ "What?" the judge roared when he regained control of himself. "How dare you use such language in a court of justice? You may leave the room until you have decided to answer civilly. Now, go!" ¶ A few minutes later the meek young man returned to the stand. ¶ "Now, what were these people doing behind the bushes in the park?" the judge demanded. ¶ The poet began to recite slowly:

"His pants were open, his prick was bare
His cock was sticking 'way out there
He put it in—you know where
If that wasn't fucking, I wasn't there!"

·225·

This would be their first night together and she was bashful. She asked her newly acquired husband after he had undressed, "John, would you mind stepping into the other room while I undress, I'm a little ashamed." ¶ So John stepped into the next room, and, as she didn't call him in ten minutes, he returned to find her apparently asleep. ¶ Looking around he found the following note: "The vaseline is on the mantel; the shoe horn on the shelf; I saw that great big thing of yours and I chloroformed myself."

·226·

LINES TO FANNY HILL

Joyous maiden, open cunted,
Who on all days keenly hunted
Hardened pricks of good proportions,
How did you elude abortions?

Prithee, Miss Hill, oh tell me now
How you could thus your swains allow
With push and prod to shoot their load
Nor hatch a bastard a la mode?

What contraceptives did you know,
That in your book no douches flow?
Were they sponges and cocoa oils
That saved you thus from Nature's toils?

Tell me, Fanny, oh, tell me, pray,
How you could fuck from day to day
Nor ever for your follies pay?

·227·

An easterner had been in a western mining town on business for some time, and feeling the urge of sex, asked a business acquaintance what they did out there in the way of female entertainment. ¶ "To tell you the truth, we have no women out here at all. The thing to do," whispered the acquaintance, "is to use a Chinaman." ¶ The easterner was shocked, but decided there was nothing else to do, and requested his friend to make the necessary arrangements. ¶ "But remember," he said, "this must be kept a secret. No one back home must know about it or I will be ruined." ¶ "I'll do the best I can, but I can't avoid letting at least five people know about it." ¶ "My God, who are the five people?" ¶ "Well, there's you, of course, and myself and the Chinaman." ¶ "And who are the other two?" ¶ "Oh, the other two men will hold the Chinaman."

·228·

Mrs. Olisbos was so very fond of her cat that she ordered an autopsy when it died. ¶ "We found," reported the coroner, "that a great number of short, curly hairs had matted in the stomach, causing an obstruction of the intestine." ¶ "Oh dear," sobbed the desolate widow, "now I know what killed poor Mr. Olisbos."

·229·

Marius entered a swimming race up the river Seine past Paris, and his adherents were surprised to find that he did not even appear at the finish line. Investigating they found him entertaining a sensuous blonde at a riverside bistrôt. He explained: ¶ "As I was starting off I looked up to see this beauty seated on the bank with no panties on. That gave me such a terrible hard-on that my cock stuck in the river bed and I had to give up the race." ¶ "Why didn't you turn over and float for a while?" ¶ "The bridges over the Seine are too low."

·230·

"About 100 miles off the coast," said Marius, "the ship sank and I alone was left afloat, in nothing but my undershirt." ¶ "Don't tell us that you swam the distance safely." ¶ "No. I just thought of my sweetheart, as I floated on my back. Then, using my cock as a mast and my shirt for sail I made 20 knots and reached Marseilles in five hours." ¶ "But how could you steer?" ¶ "I shoved my thumb up my ass and used my hand as a rudder."

·231·

When a country gentleman found he had married a girl who had lost her virginity, he was furious and inquired, "Why didn't you tell me about this? Who was your lover? That's all I want to know, who was he?" ¶ "Don't get excited, dear, it happened when my cock-eyed sister was giving me an enema."

·232·
IVY COLLEGE YELL

Root-a-dee-toot. Root-a-dee-toot
We are the girls of the Institute
All night long we prostitute
Not there, not there, not there, THERE
Faster, faster, faster
I'm coming, I'm coming, I'm coming
BANG!
Pay up!

·233·

A Sunday School teacher was showing off her class to a visiting bishop, and, fearing that some of her none-too-bright pupils might fail to reply promptly to her questions she decided to jolt their memories with the aid of a safety pin. So she stood in back of each pupil as she questioned them, jabbing them into action. ¶ "Now, Willie," she began, "who made Adam and Eve?" ¶ "God!" cried out Willie, as he felt the prick of the pin. ¶ "Splendid," nodded the bishop. ¶ The teacher moved over to another scholar. ¶ "Johnny," she said, "who was the son of God?" Johnny looked puzzled and she gave him a sharp jab. ¶ "Jesus Christ!" he cried out. ¶ "Your class is well informed," beamed the bishop. ¶ Anna, a little girl in pigtails who was next in line, had been observing the teacher's actions with frightened eyes. ¶ "Anna," said the teacher, crouching behind her, "tell us what Eve said to Adam in the garden of Eden." ¶ Anna leaped aside, just in time. ¶ "Don't you stick that thing in me!" she screamed.

·234·

Little Alfred saw his mother undressed one day, and asked, "Mother, what is that crack between your legs?" ¶ "That is where your father hit me with the axe, darling." ¶ "Jeese mom, he almost caught you in the cunt, didn't he?"

·235·

A noted prodder, suddenly discovering himself impotent, rushed to a doctor and demanded aid. The medico gave him a potion to take, warning him that he must place it in his food and that he must be careful not to miss a meal. ¶ The next night the patient was invited to a banquet and, not wishing to be questioned about his medicine, he privately instructed the waiter to place the proper amount in his soup. The other guests were all served with soup and completed their course, while the impatient medicine-taker waited and waited. Finally he excused himself and rushed out to see his waiter. ¶ "Where is my soup?" he demanded." ¶ "I put the medicine in, sir, and I'm waiting for the noodles to lay down," was the reply.

·236·

What is the difference between a girl in a bathtub, and a preacher on the pulpit? ¶ The preacher has his soul full of hope. The girl has a hole . . .

·237·

An old man was about to leave a whore and said, "I'll be back in three months." ¶ She answered, "Old reprobate, don't you think of anything except cunt."

·238·

A movie troupe was on location, doing a Garden of Eden scene. The leading lady came out to do her stuff. ¶ "Prop boy," yelled the director, "go get Miss Bigstar a bigger fig leaf."

·239·

One chap asked another: "Which would you rather do, lay with a woman or have a wet dream?" ¶ "The first," was the prompt reply. ¶ "Not me," retorted the other. "I'd rather have a wet dream. I meet nicer people that way."

·240·

An unwell whore was taking on a farmer, so when the light was put out she removed her protective sponge and placed it on the table next to the bed. He in turn took out his chew of tobacco and put it on the same table. When they were finished, she picked up the tobacco and stuck it up her vagina and he put the sponge in his mouth and began to chew. ¶ When the tobacco began to burn she said, "You bastard, I think you've given me syphilis." ¶ Just then he spit, and seeing the blood said, "Don't complain, you son-of-a-bitch, you've given me consumption."

·241·

The big attraction at the Fair was a cow that was reputed to be worth a million dollars. "Why," queried one of the farmers, "is that there cow worth so much money?" ¶ "Because, if you step up here real close, you will notice that she has a pussy just like a woman's." ¶ The farmer stepped up, examined the cow closely and suddenly burst out into roars of laughter. He continued to roar for fully five minutes, holding his stomach while the tears were rolling down his face. ¶ When finally he quieted down, they asked him what he saw so funny about the cow, to which he replied, "And to think that I got a woman with a pussy like a cow, and it ain't worth a nickel."

·242·

The professor of travel at a famous university had just returned from a tour around the world and the students crowded around eager to question him. ¶ "Where did you find the dirtiest place in the world?" asked one. ¶ "The promenade," answered the professor. ¶ "Where is the promenade?" ¶ "The promenade is the space between a woman's ass and her cunt, where the crabs have to walk on stilts to keep from getting their feet in the shit."

·243·

A Frenchman, noticed, in a hotel room across the way from his house, a beautiful woman walking around naked. The blood ran to his prick and he ran across to the hotel and up the stairs opening his pants as he went. He came to a room with the door ajar and a naked body lying on the bed. He rushed into the room, tore off his pants and went to work on the body, which was that of a man who had just finished shaving and lay on his stomach to rest. ¶ The hotel guest awoke in a fright to feel the prick of his countryman stuck all the way up his ass. Angered at not being asked permission for taking such privileges, he picked up the razor from the table and with one clean sweep, severed the prick of his ill mannered countryman to the hilt. ¶ "Call ze surgeon, call ze surgeon," yelled the bleeding Frenchman. ¶ "To hell wiz ze surgeon," cried the other. "Bring me ze cork-screw, queek."

·244·

An English officer riding through the park in full regalia, red uniform, boots and horse equally polished and cape flying gracefully in the gentle breeze, came upon a young girl sitting on a bench alongside the bridle path. He stopped in front of her and she exclaimed, "What a beautiful 'Orse you 'ave there." ¶ This compliment made the officer feel very superior and he did not answer, but looked in the other direction as if something more interesting were going on. ¶ "My, what a beautiful uniform you 'as on," said the young girl. ¶ Still the officer did not turn his head. But just then the horse spread his hind legs and took a piss which splattered all over the girl. ¶ "I can't sye I think very much of your 'orse, but you're still a fine man." she said. ¶ He turned around slowly but still keeping his head high, said, "I 'opes next time we meets under better 'orse-pisses."

·245·

A small repertory was playing a little town in the north-west. Shows, being very rare in this part of the world, the lumberjacks turned out in full force to see 'Macbeth,' which the company had selected for the opening night. ¶ Everything was going along beautifully, the timber men having refrained from comment for half an hour. Then the line "What shall we do with the body?" was spoken. ¶ "Fuck it before it gets too cold!" came from the gallery, and as the entire house was thrown into chaos, it was impossible to continue the play. ¶ The next morning the sheriff met the travelling thespians, bag and baggage, headed for the railway station. He apologized on behalf of the town for what had happened on the previous night and induced the company to give another performance that night, saying, "I wants dese boys to get ejucated to the finer things in life. But don't start with this, what do you call him, Shakespeare guy. Give de bums sometin' lighter and we'll gradually work up, an I'll be there per-sonally to keep order, get me?" ¶ As advised, the program was of a lighter nature that night. For three quarters of an hour the show went on without a sound from the audience. The sheriff sat in a box near the stage, facing the audience, with a big six shooter held in each hand and in view of all. A puny little actor was reading a poem included in his part, which ran: "Oh, what is more beautiful than a woman's breasts." ¶ Just then the sheriff made one leap from the box to the stage, pointed the guns at the crowded audience and shouted, "I'll empty both these guns into the first son-of-a-bitch that says cunt."

·246·

The stingiest Scotchman is the one who slept with his mother-in-law, to save the 'wear and tear' on his pretty wife.

·247·

After completing his examination, the doctor informed the young woman he had discovered the cause of her discomforts. ¶ "Go home," he said, "and tell your husband to prepare for a baby." ¶ "I haven't any husband," she replied. ¶ "Then tell your lover." ¶ "But I haven't any lover. I never had one." ¶ "Then tell your mother to prepare for the second coming of Jesus."

·248·

Two gays were having their pictures taken together. "Do you want it mounted?" asked the photographer. ¶ "No, this time we'll have it taken shaking hands."

·249·

When they left the photographers, the same two were waiting for an elevator. ¶ "Going down?" asked the operator. ¶ "Not yet, dear, we were just discussing it."

·250·

Mr. Rosenbaum caught his son Jakie jerking off. He gave him a dollar, told him where the whore house was and said, "Here's feefty cents more. Stop in de drug store, buy a condrum and de man vill tell you how to put it on." ¶ Jakie went to the drug store as advised, purchased a condrum and the clerk showed him graphically how to use it by putting it on his thumb and rolling it down. ¶ The madam of the whore house, a German lady, seeing that Jake was young, innocent, and Jewish, took this opportunity to give Sylvia 'The Syph' a break, as none of the regular customers would have her on account of her disease. ¶ "Have you a condrum?" asked Sylvia. ¶ "Sure," said Jake. ¶ "Well, I'll put out the light and get ready while you put it on." ¶ When they had finished fucking, Sylvia said, "That condrum must have broken, I feel all wet." ¶ Jake held up his thumb on which reposed the condrum and said, "No, it didn't break. It's just as good as when I put it on."

·251·

 stands for Anus
The invert's delight;
The back door of wisdom,
The pederast's rite.
All joys, say the gays
Seem flaccid and stale
Compared to the thrill of
Their own brand of "tail."

·252·

 stands for Bugger
The rogue of the field.
The ass, bitch and ewe lamb
He forces to yield.
Levitical statutes
Mean nothing to him . . .
He'd trade any girl for
A friendly mule's quim.

·253·

 stands for Coint-juice
That nectarine flow
Which diligent drilling
Brings forth from below.
When this divine ichor
Flows fresh from the tap
The bird who won't sample
Is plainly a sap.

·254·

 stands for Danglers
More coarsely termed nuts,
So dear to the heart of
Sedate dames and sluts.
An asset in bed play
Their beauty enthralls,
But it's not so much fun to
Get kicked in the balls.

·255·

 stands for Eunuch
The safest of men;
This chap is no rooster,
He's more like a hen.
Devoid of a ramrod
He guards the Sult's flocks;
And wallows in pure thoughts,
As plump as an ox.

·256·

 stands for Farter—
How tuneful his ass—
Delighting his friends with
Its volleys of gas.
He needs no pianist
No uke, drum or harp,
His solo notes cover
Low C to A sharp.

·257·

 stands for Gism,
The grandest of goos,
Gelatinous gravy,
Omnipotent ooze!
It shoots from the bungs of
All vertebrate cocks,
And breeds the most varied
Of domestic stocks.

·258·

 stands for Hole-space:
Some Indian squaws
Possess enough room for
At least three papaws.
And dames with sufficient
Square inches of snatch
Bring perfume and jewels home
With never a catch.

·259·

 stands for Inches
The one simple test
Applied by the wench who
Is out for the best.
Though Bonaparte's musket
Was well under four
Unless you show twice that
You'll get no encore.

·260·

 stands for Jockstrap
To hold up the plums;
For gents made of lamb's wool
And horsehide for bums.
Oh, many a poor egg
At tennis or track
Has dropped half a testis
For lack of a sack.

stands for Knobbies,
Like pumpkins they grow,
And droop o'er the valley
That's spread out below.
These carnal contraptions
Designed for the young
Are prized by old coots with
Naught left but a tongue.

 stands for Lapper,
Who reaps as he sows
With Ph.D. tongue and
A "sixty-nine" pose.
This twotch titillator
Is much in demand;
He cleans up the kitchen
And thinks that it's grand.

·263·

 stands for Mink-turd,
The vilest of snot.
"Eat a plate for a million?"
No, thanks, rather not.
They talk about camel dung,
Goose shit and such,
But an adult mink's load
Can't be outstunk by much.

·264·

 stands for Nooky,
The tired workman's joy.
Just cover the face and
Think: "Helen of Troy."
Though dopes go ill-clothed and
They let their meals slump,
All mankind insists on
Its tri-weekly hump.

stands for Odor
The most fragrant rise
From nubian snatches
And balinese thighs.
The impotent diddler
Finds life's greatest thrill
Just catching the scents at
The base of the hill.

 stands for Pecker—
The Horn of Affright—
A drain pipe by day and
A weapon by night.
Some peters are nut-brown
Some grey and some red,
It's reach and not color
They look for in bed.

·267·

 stands for Quickee,
A rapid-fire shot;
Great stuff for the back seat
Or studio cot.
No time wasted bussing
Or tickling the dick
Just undo the breeches
And plunge in the prick.

·268·

 stands for Rhino
The fuckingest beast,
All day long he bellows
"Aw, gimme a piece't!"
His wang's half a yard long
His balls weigh like lead
The females take one look
Then just drop and spread.

·269·

 stands for Screwing
Victorian way,
The time-tested posture
Lewd minds call a 'lay.'
It's true it's old-fashioned,
The smart set says "nix,"
But they all come back to it
When tired of new tricks.

·270·

 stands for Taffy
The candy of sin;
Bad uncles present it
And nieces give in.
It serves to stuff coozies,
A hard pseudo-tool,
In many a convent
And girl's boarding-school.

·271·

 stands for Urine,
 Low bards call it piss,
 Majestically spurting
 From each mare's whatsis.
 This aureate liquid
 Is bottled and hid,
 And passed off as pop to
 Some ignorant kid.

·272·

 stands for Virgin
 There aren't many left.
 In all of New York there's
 Not one mothy cleft.
 Good-bye to the days of
 Untupped quiffs and quims;
 A hymen at eighteen
 Now brings forth church hymns.

·273·

 is Widow,
Three boxed for four bits.
The Boy Scouts all have 'em
In safety first kits.
Some classy shops feature
Fish hides for a buck—
They break just the same, and
You're shit out of luck.

·274·

 marks the spot where
The itching begins;
Sometimes on the joy-stick,
Sometimes on the shins.
Sometimes it's the clap and
Again it's the gleet.
The worst place to get it's
The base of your seat.

·275·

 stands for Yanker,
The self-driving chap.
He greases his pole and
Provokes his own sap.
Absolved of the need of
A quarrelsome wife
He humps himself nightly
And lives a great life.

·276·

 stands for zipper,
For setting her free,
Stripping her nude,
Her fair form to see.
Clothes were sewn by fools like me,
But only God can make a she.

•277•

A man went to the house of an old friend to dinner. A terrific storm broke out and it was decided that he spend the night with his old friend, and the old friend's gorgeous wife. ¶ As there was no spare bed in the house, he was forced to sleep with them. The old friend slept in the middle, his wife on one side and the visitor on the other. ¶ After the husband was asleep, the wife motioned the visitor to come over on her side of the bed. ¶ "I couldn't think of doing such a thing. He is my oldest friend." he whispered. "And besides he would be certain to wake up." ¶ "Nothing in the world will wake him, I'm sure of that," said she. ¶ "But certainly, if I go over there and screw you, he will waken." ¶ "I tell you he won't. Pull a hair out of his ass-hole and see if that wakes him." ¶ The visitor did as he was bidden and sure enough the husband remained asleep. So he climbed over to the wife's side of the bed and gave her the works. When he had finished he climbed back to his own side, but he wasn't there long before she beckoned to him again, and again he pulled out a hair to determine if his old friend was asleep. This went on for fifteen times during the night. Each time he screwed the woman he pulled out one of the ass-hole hairs of her husband. ¶ The sixteenth time he pulled a hair, the husband awoke and said, "I don't mind you screwing my wife, but for Christ's sake stop using my ass for a score-board."

•278•

A prominent man, was dying and called his son and two daughters to his bedside. "Children," he said, "I want to inform you that I never married your mother." He then passed on. ¶ The children sat around in solemn amazement. Suddenly the son rose and said to his sisters: "I don't know what you two bastards are doing, but here is one son-of-a-bitch who's going to the movies."

·279·

Two tramps stopped outside a lewd woman's cottage. Lionel knocked on the door and asked for something to eat. A buxom wench asked him in. On the kitchen table was a plate with two ears of corn. The wench told him he was welcome to them if he screwed her. ¶ She went into the bedroom and as he followed, he grabbed one ear of the corn which he used for the job too distasteful for his prick. Returning to the kitchen he replaced the used ear of corn and ate the other one. ¶ When he came out his buddy Archibald asked how he had made out. "All right," he replied. "You go in too." ¶ Archibald did so. He screwed the wench and ate the remaining ear of corn. ¶ Joining his colleague, he was asked, "How was it?" ¶ "The corn was fine," he answered, "but the butter was rancid."

·280·

Willie, just coming of age, asked his father, if he could have a piece of tail. "Sure, Willie," said the father, "Here's a dollar. Go to the village and get it." ¶ On the way Willie met his grandmother who asked where he was going. "I'm going to the village to get a piece of tail. Pop gave me a dollar." ¶ The grandmother said, "Give me the dollar and do it to me." They went into the bushes and Willie performed the act. ¶ Returning home, his father asked if he had gotten his piece. "Yes," Willie replied, "I met grandma on the way and she said to give her the dollar and do it to her. Which I did." ¶ "What!" yelled the father, "You little bastard, you screwed my mother?" ¶ "Sure," said Willie, "Didn't you screw mine?"

·281·

Ode to a Mother
'Twixt the heat of the prick,
And the prickly heat,
Baby sucking me,
And John fucking me—
I'm just no good.

·282·

A mother invited three prospective husbands for her daughter to her place in the country. The object of the invitation was to find which of the three was the most suitable; so she put them all together in the room next to the one she and her daughter occupied that night. The partition was very thin and they could hear all that was going on. ¶ Said one man to the other, "You know Jack, when my father dies next year, I shall inherit a half million dollars." ¶ "That's the one you're going to marry," said the mother to the daughter. ¶ "That's nothing," said one of the others, "My father is eighty years old now, and when he dies I shall inherit several millions." ¶ "That's the man for you," said mother. ¶ "Get off my cock, Jack," said the third. ¶ "I'm not on your cock," answered Jack. ¶ "Well if you're not on it, it's over you and Al is on it." ¶ "That's the man for me," said the daughter.

·283·

A man went to bed with an old woman and her two daughters. In order to protect the daughters she put a gun under her pillow. ¶ During the night, one of the daughters beckoned to the man. He whispered to her that he was afraid of the gun reclining under the pillow. "Don't worry," she answered, "It isn't loaded." So he gave her the works. ¶ Soon the same thing happened with the second daughter, and again he said he was afraid of the gun. "Don't worry, it isn't loaded," she said. He then gave her the works. ¶ This happened about four times before the mother woke up and beckoned to the man to get on top of her. He pointed to the pillow under which the gun lay. "It isn't loaded," said the mother. "Neither is this," said the man pointing to his prick.

·284·

What is it that goes in hard and stiff and comes out soft and wet? ¶ Chewing gum.

·285·

"Madam, I have just arrived in town and shall be here for six months. I want the tightest girl in the whore house, and, if I am satisfied, shall return many times." ¶ The madam, not having any such thing as a tight girl in the place, went upstairs and whispered to Maizie, "Put some alum up your cunt. That will make it very tight and this guy will get a good lay." ¶ Maizie did as she was ordered, and when the stranger came down again the madam asked, "Well sir, how did you like it, was it tight enough?" ¶ Between compressed lips he answered, "Yes madam, very good."

·286·

A German girl, who had not been in this country very long, got a job as a maid in a rich woman's home. One night while a gay party was in progress the madam entered the maid's room and found a condrum on the floor. Before she could speak, the maid said, "I quit this job." ¶ "Why?" asked the madam. "Weren't you ever jazzed when you worked as a maid in Germany?" ¶ "Yes, but in Germany they don't jazz until the skin comes off," she said pointing to the condrum.

·287·

A gypsy phrenologist on MacDougal street numbers many Greenwich Village celebrities among her clients. One night when she was unwell she asked one of these celebrities, "Did you ever get your palm read?" ¶ "No," he replied, "I don't believe in that sort of thing." ¶ "Well then you'd better take your hand from under my skirt," was the rejoinder.

·288·

The life of a broker: 1929, follies girl and a yacht. 1930, whore and a canoe. 1931, water wings and a hard on.

·289·

The scene is a western bar. All the miners are standing around listening to a tirade from Phoebe, the leading whore of the town. She climaxed her remarks by banging on the bar with her clenched fist. ¶ "I've known you all, man and boy, for going-on-to five years and all that time I've never been fucked right once. If you need encouragement I'll give you some. Here's a hundred dollars in new bills for any man who can make me come tonight." ¶ With this she flounced up the rickety stairs to her room and leaning over the balcony with her thumb to her nose, she let out a final lusty raspberry. ¶ The group stood about in shame-faced silence. After a pause up spoke the little Irishman, Shorty Magraw, 4 foot 2. ¶ "Begorra, I think I'll take a chance at that." This was met with peals of laughter. ¶ "What can you do with your lousy 3 1/2 inches?" ¶ None the less he made his way up the stairs to Phoebe's room. ¶ The crowd waited, five, ten, fifteen minutes. Suddenly they looked up to see Shorty descending the stairs, busily counting the bills of the hundred dollar roll. ¶ "How did you do it Shorty, with your 3 1/2 inches?" ¶ "Wall, I'll tell you boys. I tried everything but I couldn't make it go off 'till I puecked in it."

·290·

A gay lark paid his usual Saturday night visit to his favorite whore house. When he arrived all the girls were busy, but rather than turn him away he was directed to the top floor to the small room on the left. He groped around in the dark, finally felt warm flesh and proceeded. ¶ After the customary number of jabs he released a warm flow. While resting from his exertions he perceived a most disagreeable odor. "For Christ's sake what stinks?" he inquired. ¶ A very old and feeble voice answered. "Sir, they pressed me into service to-night and really I am too old to come, so I just shit."

·291·

"What color is blood?" asked Pat of Mike as they were being chased by a regiment of German soldiers, the bullets whistling by their ears. ¶ "Yours is yellow," answered Mike. ¶ Pat put his hand on the back of his pants, looked at it and said, "Begorra, I've been wounded."

·292·

Bill and Vinnie, two tennis stars, were playing a match. They came up to the net to change courts. ¶ "Say, Vinnie, look at that charming red headed dame in the stands. Do you notice that the hair on her cunt is black?" ¶ "I will look Bill, when I get over to your end." ¶ They changed courts again. "Did you see it, Vinnie?" ¶ "Yeh, Bill, but her cunt hair isn't black, that's just a collection of flies on it."

·293·

A small towner had just been married and spent his first night in a large New York hotel. In the morning he approached the clerk and asked what he owed. The clerk informed him "Two dollars a piece." The rube laid down a twenty dollar bill and departed.

·294·

Mike and Pat were strolling through one of the side streets when they were called by a trollop in the window. "Come on in boys," she invited, "and let me show you a few tricks." ¶ Mike hesitated, but Pat, always ready for anything went inside. The whore had an egg in her hand when Pat made his entrance. Overcome by his fire Pat rushed to the battle. The whore had no opportunity to dispose of the egg, so just dropped it into her cunt. Pat worked like hell, when suddenly, looking down, he saw the yellow mess running down her legs. Frightened, he jumped off the dame, dove through the window and yelled to Mike. "For Christ sake Mike, run like hell. I am after busting her shit bladder."

·295·

The captain of a boat was horrified when he caught some of the sailors buggering one another. In order to stop this practice, he purchased some small barrels, bored holes into them and gave them to the boys for sexual pleasure. ¶ When the ship returned from a long voyage, the barrels were full of semen, and the Scotch captain decided it would be a good idea to sell it for wax. He made a bargain with a man and sold the entire lot profitably. ¶ The next time he returned from a long voyage, he went to see the man about selling him another load of tallow. The man cursed and swore calling him a swindling son-of-a-bitch. "I made candles from dat last bunch you sold me, and now I'm ruined." ¶ "How come?" asked the captain. ¶ "I sold dem to a convent, and efferybody in de place got babies."

·296·

Pat gazed in wonder at the first pile of grapefruit he had ever seen. "Shure, what are those?" he asked. ¶ The vegetable dealer saw an opportunity for some fun. "Why those are elephant eggs." he replied. ¶ "Elephant eggs! Shure what do you do with them?" ¶ "Why, simply take one home, lay on it for twenty-four hours and you will hatch an elephant. Sell it to the circus and by repeating this you can become wealthy." ¶ "Shure that's a grand idea, give me one." ¶ Pat hustled home terribly excited. "Mary! Mary!" he yelled, "our fortune is made." After a hurried explanation he peeled off his clothes. ¶ "Let me get to bed quick and lay on this egg." Mary assisted him to bed and placed the grapefruit gently under his stomach. ¶ She then ran to the neighbors and told them the glad news. The widow Clancy insisted upon proof. Mary took her into the bedroom and told her to put her hand under Mike and feel the egg. ¶ She did and after groping a few minutes jumped back and yelled, "By golly he's right, it's hatching already. Sure I felt its trunk."

·297·

In an impoverished family it was necessary for three small children to sleep in the same bed with their parents. It was a cold room and the children all wore hats when put to bed. This night the old man was feeling his oats and started screwing the old lady. Suddenly after one particularly strenuous jab down came the bed and on the floor landed the three kids minus the hats. Everything was finally adjusted and the kids put back to bed with their hats on. The old boy started again when he thought the youngsters were asleep to complete his job. Again the bed broke and again down came the kids and off flew the hats. Back they went again, with their hats on. After a wait for the kids to get to sleep the performance started again with the same result. After about five attempts he waited a while longer, and started again. He had just got into his stride when suddenly one of the kids yelled, "Hold your hats, boys, here we go again."

·298·

Jacobson, on his return from a business trip of several weeks' duration, became suspicious that his wife had been untrue during his absence. At first she denied it, but finally, under his persistent questioning, admitted she had "stepped out." ¶ "Who was it?" demanded Jacobson. Mrs. Jacobson's only response was a fresh flood of tears. ¶ "Vas it Finklestein?" ¶ "No." ¶ "Vas it Cohen?" ¶ "No." ¶ "Vas it Eisenstein?" ¶ "No." ¶ "Vas it Gold-stein?" ¶ "No." ¶ "Vas it Sapiro?" ¶ "No." ¶ "Vas it Perlmutter?" ¶ "No." ¶ Jacobson cogitated a moment. "So," he said, finally, "none of my friends iss good enough for you, huh?"

·299·

Sour milk song: Bum titie, bum titie, bum titie bum.

·300·

A travelling saleswoman stopped at a farmer's house. The farmer's wife had retired early, leaving the farmer alone with the saleslady. "Why don't you do something, Hiram?" asked the lady. Some time passed and as nothing happened, she lifted her skirts further, and said, "Oh, Hiram, please come on and do something." ¶ Hiram took out his harmonica and played 'Yankee-Doodle'.

·301·

A lonely cow-boy, who hadn't been fucked in a long time, was riding on a range in New Mexico when he came upon a band of Indians wrapped in blankets. With one leap he was off his horse and on to the nearest Indian. ¶ "Me buck, me buck," said the Indian, meaning that he was a male. ¶ "I don't give a damn if you do," said the cow-puncher. "I ride 'em bucking or not."

·302·

"Stop the car," she said, "I have to take a shit." ¶ "Go over there and shit over the edge of that cliff," said her companion. ¶ She didn't return for some time so he went to get her. "Look," she said, "what I did! I shit right in that canoe down there!" ¶ "That's no canoe. That's a reflection of your cunt."

·303·

The main event at Mrs. Astorbilt's party, was the village idiot, who masturbated his huge tool in the middle of the floor, to the joy of the encircled onlookers. He masturbated for some time and the guests began to get impatient and shouted, "Why don't you come?" As that didn't help one man threw a quarter at his feet, thinking this would rush the issue. Another followed suit, and still another, making the kitty seventy-five cents. ¶ "One dollar," said the idiot. "One dollar, one dollar, o—n—e d—o—ll—ar. All right, let 'er go for seventy-five."

·304·

It is said, that at one of the old time festival and field days, held in England at her Majesty's command, one of the favorite knights, named Colonel Bahue, was creating great furor with his feats of strength. They do say that when the colonel was stripped to the buff he was seen to be a man of tremendous proportions. He would grab his polywog in his left hand and after giving it a few deft cuffs it soon arose to its normal state of rigidity. He then placed a scuttle of coal upon it and paraded the arena to the plaudits of the multitude. Suddenly Michael O'Dowd, the Irish challenger, not to be outdone, jumped from the grand stand to the center of the arena, and, placing his prick up Colonel Bahue's ass carried both the colonel and the scuttle of coal, while the good Queen split her gloves applauding.

·305·

We played before the King of England who bestowed medals on our breasts according to the size of the instrument we played. There was Joe with his harp and there was Frank with his bass drum and there was I with my damned little piccolo. ¶ We played before the King of Kokomo and he ordered our instruments stuck up our asses. And there was Joe with his harp and there was Frank with his big bass drum and there was I with my dear little piccolo.

·306·

A travelling salesman was staying at a farm house and naturally he had the farmer's daughter. Being unable to buy condrums in the vicinity, he used a silk handkerchief instead. ¶ He returned a year later to find the girl had given birth to a son. "He's a fine boy," the farmer was telling the salesman. ¶ "Well he ought to be," was the reply, "I strained him through a silk handkerchief."

·307·

One night one of her men asked an apparently young whore how old she was. ¶ "What difference does that make?" replied the dame. ¶ "Oh just curious. I know you're young, but just how old are you?" ¶ "Well if you must know, I'm sixteen." ¶ "Now listen," replied the customer, "I know you're young but don't kid me. Why you couldn't get those drawers that filthy in only sixteen years."

·308·

Two Jewish travellers stopped at a hotel and asked for a room. They were informed by the clerk that all he had left was a small room with a single bed. Nothing else available, they accepted it. Abe woke up suddenly, tapped Moe, and said. "Moe, don't answer me now, but by any chance are you sucking me off?"

·309·

The German army was lined up for inspection before Chancelor Hitler. General Georing sat on his horse next to Hitler and ordered the men: "One—pull out cock. Two—draw back foreskin. Three—piss. Four—push foreskin back to place." ¶ "Let me try it now," asked Herr Hitler, and he drilled the men thus: "Two-four. Two-four. Two-four."

·310·

A little boy was taking a pee in the cow pasture, when a calf came along and thinking the prick was a tit, began to suck it. "MAMMA, COME GET THIS CALF AWAY." shouted the boy. "Mamma, come get this calf away," he said more feebly. "Ma-mm-aa co—ome get thi—is ca—lf a—way." Then silence.

·311·

There is a report that a movie star writes all her material in bed. When asked why, she replied that she always did her best work in bed.

·312·

A modern flapper rushed into her home the other day and very excitedly asked her mother—"Ma could I have a baby?" ¶ "Why child don't be silly, of course you can't." ¶ "Are you sure Ma, I can't have a baby?" ¶ "Certainly not child." ¶ "Whoopie!" yelled the flapper.

·313·

A daughter was telling her mother the latest ways of fucking. "The way I like it best," she said, "Is to lay on the bed spread my legs as wide as possible and let Bill pump on top of me." ¶ "Good," said the mother, "I shall try that tonight with your father." ¶ The next day the daughter received word that her mother was in the hospital and rushed there to see what the trouble was. ¶ "Well," said mother, "I tried that new way of fucking last night, and they're still probing for your father."

·314·

A man took his young daughter out for a drive in their car. Out in the country he stopped the car and got out to take a piss. The daughter followed him and was watching until he looked up and chased her back to the car. ¶ "But daddy, I want to ask you a question," she insisted. "How many of those things have you, and what did you do with the great big one you stuck in mamma this morning?"

·315·

"I can't understand it," said the mother. "I've always warned you against that young man, and you persist in going with him. He's lazy, he's dissolute, and his reputation has always been bad. In short, he isn't good for you." ¶ "But, mother, he *is* good for me. You know that sickness I used to have every month? He's cured that already!"

·316·

Song of the Navy: I hate to leave my buddies behind.

Z stands for zipper.

·317·

For years Jamison had stopped at the same hotel in
one of the small towns on his route, so when, on one of
his trips, he found the place under new management, he
was reluctant to register. But the new owner assured him
the accommodations were at least as good as ever. ¶ "I'll
guarantee satisfactory service in every respect," he said.
¶ So Jamison registered. That evening he spoke confi-
dentially to the new proprietor. ¶ "Anderson, who used
to run this hotel," he said, "always provided me with a
girl to sleep with. Of course, I paid her reasonably." ¶
The new owner shook his head. ¶ "I'm afraid I can't do
that," he said. "You see, my wife's in partnership with
me, and she's very strait-laced about such things." ¶
"Very well. Then I'll go elsewhere." ¶ The hotel man
thought a minute. Then he said: ¶ "Wait. You go to your
room and I'll talk to my wife. Perhaps I can talk her out
of her strict ideas, seeing you're an old patron." ¶ But
the wife was adamant. "This is a decent hotel," she said,
"and I don't care if he is an old patron. Tell him we
won't have any such goings on." ¶ "He won't take 'no'
for an answer," responded her husband. "You'd better
tell him yourself, and that will settle it." ¶ "You bet I'll
tell him," she announced, and set off for the guest's
room. ¶ A few minutes later there was a terrific commotion at the head of the stairs, and Jamison came half-
tumbling down. His shirt was torn, his face was scratched,
and he was red and panting. ¶ "That was a tough old
bitch you sent up," he said to the hotel man, "but I
fucked her, God damn her!"

·318·

A fellow, as was his wont, was masturbating in front
of a full length mirror. Unfortunately his attempted orgy
was not crowned with success. He went soft and flat right
in the midst of his manipulations. ¶ He looked at himself
sadly in the mirror. "Well," he said, "I guess I'm just
not my type."

·319·

It was graduation day and the teacher was proudly exhibiting the knowledge of her pupils to the school board. ¶ "What is the fastest thing in the world, William?" she asked. ¶ "Thought," said William unhesitatingly. ¶ "Excellent," said the teacher, and asked Mary the same question. ¶ "Lightning," answered Mary quickly. ¶ "Very good," said the teacher, and then called on little Johnnie for the same question. ¶ "Shit," answered Johnnie instantly. ¶ Horrified the teacher took him aside and asked the meaning of such an answer. ¶ "While on the way home from school the other day," said Johnnie, "Without a thought and quicker than lightning, I shit in my pants."

·320·

During a spelling bee the teacher called on little Johnnie. ¶ "Johnnie, you spell Peter," she said. ¶ "P-E-E-T . . . Oh, I can't spell it teacher. It's too long." ¶ "Tommy, you spell Peter for us," asked the teacher. ¶ "P-E-E-T . . . I can't spell it. It's too hard." ¶ Then the teacher called on little Mary who hopped up and spelled, "P-E-T-E-R, they can't come too long and too hard for us, can they teacher?"

·321·

Two dogs were screwing on a railroad track. A fast train sped along cutting right through them. One dog had his tail cut off the other lost his head. The moral is: Never lose your head over a piece of tail.

·322·

The well-known magazine had been expecting some copy from a big writer for several days. The deadline was approaching and the editor sent an urgent message, demanding the reason for the delay. ¶ He received the following special delivery letter: "Too fucking busy, and vice versa."

·323·

Mrs. O'Murphy wanted to confess to the priest that she had been farting much of late, thinking that it was a sin. However, she did not know how to tell the preacher about it, and went to Mrs. O'Rielly for information. ¶ "Tell him," said Mrs. O'Rielly, "That ye've been commitin' adultery." ¶ "Father," said Mrs. O'Murphy, "I want to confess that I've been commitin' a lot of adultery." ¶ "How often do you do it?" asked the lord's servant. ¶ "About three-hundred and fifty times a day." she said. ¶ "What does your husband say?" asked the priest. ¶ "He says, 'more power to your big fat ass, Maggie.'"

·324·

In a Middle-Western University, a co-ed class was having an oral quiz in physiology, "And now," said the professor, "who can tell me the only member of the human body which is capable of expanding to three times its normal size?" ¶ The class fidgeted, turned red around the ears, and looked modestly into its lap. "Come, come," the professor repeated impatiently, "someone must know. What is the only part of the human body which can expand to three times its normal size? Miss Smith, you tell us! Stand up!" ¶ But Miss Smith faltered, turned pale, and finally gasped out that she didn't know. At which the professor, furious, raised his voice and proclaimed, "Very well, then, *I'll* tell you! The only member of the human body capable of expanding to three times its normal size is the pupil of the eye. . . . And as for *you*, Miss Smith, *you're* nothing but an idle dreamer!"

·325·

A man came running up to a cop in Central Park and said, "Officer, I've just been insulted by a couple of fairies a few benches down the line." ¶ "If you don't like our dear park you don't have to sthay," lisped the cop.

·326·

We all make mistakes, that's why there are so many children.

·327·

A man came into an employment agency looking very dejected. ¶ "I thought I got you a job with a lady writer yesterday," said the clerk. ¶ "You did sir," said the man with the short prick. "I was hired, fucked and fired in an hour."

·328·

An ex-whore went to a large store and wanted to have her purchases sent. After getting the street address, the clerk, in the approved store manner, said: "141 West 23rd St., Manhattan. Is that a *house*, madam?" ¶ "No!!" she shrieked, "It's *not* a house! and DON'T CALL ME MADAM!"

·329·

Said Mandy to Sandy, "Do you love me honey, or is that a jack-knife I feel in your pocket?"

·330·

"What's the difference between the Twentieth Century Limited and a man with twelve children?" ¶ "The Twentieth Century Limited always pulls out on time."

·331·

"Would you believe it, Al, my four year old son knocked up the maid." ¶ "A four year old boy? Why that's impossible man." ¶ "Yes sir, the little son-of-a-bitch punctured all my condrums with a pin."

·332·

An Englishman saw his wife fucked before his eyes by a Frenchman without making a move. ¶ "What's the idea, why didn't you say a word?" ¶ "What could I say, I don't know a word of French."

·333·

An English matron, who claimed direct lineage to William The Conqueror, was giving final words of instruction to her daughter Cynthia, about to be married. ¶ "Always remember, that it's the most unspeakable, reprehensible physical act in the world," she concluded. ¶ "But mother dear, you've had six children. If it's as bad as all that, how could you possibly have gone through with it?" ¶ "I closed my eyes and thought of England."

·334·

Shamus O'Flaherty, was screwing a whore for all he was worth. To his horror, he suddenly found the girl limp in his arms, and soon enough discovered that she had died in his embrace. ¶ The incident was reported to the police and Shamus was brought before the Sergeant. ¶ "It's true sergeant, I was takin' me pleasure in a cat house, and I'm not denyin' the poor girl's dead, God rest her soul." ¶ "How did it happen?" asked the sergeant. ¶ "I had my hand over her ass-hole, two pounds of cock down her cunt, and my tongue down her throat, and how the hell the breath of life got out of her, is a mystery to me."

·335·

A Texas man went to a lawyer and told the attorney he wanted an injunction against his wife. ¶ "What kind of an injunction?" asked the lawyer. ¶ "I don't know what kind of injunction," the fellow replied. "That's what I came to you for. She's fucking all over the place." ¶ "Oh, I see," said the lawyer. "What you want is a divorce." ¶ No sir," said the chap. "I don't want no divorce. I want an injunction. That woman's the best piece of tail in the State of Texas."

·336·

Here's to the king! What king? Fuc-king.

·337·

Two Indian chiefs, Little Bear and Big Wind, had saved up enough money on the happy hunting ground to make a trip to the big city. ¶ They went to one of the finest hotels and were shown to their room by a bell-hop. "Here is your bed, and here is the bath, and here is the water," the boy informed them before he left the room. ¶ Soon after, a shot was heard and the house detective ran up to the Indian's room. He rushed into the toilet, and, lying next to the bowl in a pool of blood was chief Big Wind, shot through his large Indian heart. ¶ Chief Little Bear stood over the body with his arms crossed. ¶ "Did you kill him?" the detective asked. ¶ "Um, me killum. Heah no good. Him shit in spring."

·338·

Two hill-billies were up before the judge for disturbing the peace. One of them had a black eye and was trying to explain. ¶ "I didn' do nothin', Judge," he pleaded. "Honest, I didn' do nothin'. I was just a-walkin' over by the railroad track las' Sat'day night when all of a sudden I steps on somethin', an' then somethin' hits me, and I swear t' God, Judge, I don't know nothin' more about it. I swears I don't, Judge." ¶ "And what have you got to say?" said the Judge, turning to the other prisoner. ¶ "Well, you sees, Judge, it was this way. I takes that new pretty gal out walkin' las' Sat'day night, and we just natcherly wanders down by the railroad tracks. Well, Judge, then we jus' natcherly gets to messin' aroun', and I says to her, 'How much?' And she says, 'A dollar a inch.' Well, Judge, that's a lot of money and I only has two dollars, but I says 'All right.' And so help me, Judge, I was tryin' my best to be an honest man and keep within my means, so to speak, when along comes this son-of-a-bitch and steps on me, and done run my bill up to fo'teen dollars! An' that's why I hit him, Judge, he done run my bill up to fo'teen dollars!"

·339·

Said the egg to the water—"How do you expect me to get hard, if you don't get hot?"

·340·

A young couple were watching an X-rated screen effort. ¶ Suddenly they found they had pissed in each others' hand.

·341·

A demure miss was seated on her boy-friend's lap, tightly grasping his cock. ¶ "What's your father's business?" he asked. ¶ "My father's a billposter." she replied, without relaxing her hold. ¶ "Well, here comes some paste for him."

·342·

An old man was, as it were, fucking a girl. Tired of supporting his weight, the young slut said professionally, "If you can't come, write."

·343·

Little Willie had a very bad habit of biting his finger nails. His mother was desperately trying to effect a cure. On a street car one day they sat opposite a pregnant woman. "See," said Willie's mother, "if you don't stop biting your nails, you will get a great big stomach like that lady." ¶ Willie looked so intently at the lady, that he aroused her attention. She leaned over to him and asked, "Young man, why do you stare at me that way?" ¶ "Because," said Willie, "I know what *you've* been doing."

·344·

A toast to heat:
Not the heat that burns down shanties,
But the heat that turns down panties.

·345·

Olga, a Swedish housemaid, got a position with an elderly lady who treated her very well except that she exercised a rigorous oversight of Olga's goings and comings, particularly on the maid's evenings out. On those occasions, after Olga's return, she exacted from the maid a full and circumstantial account of where she had been, and with whom. Also she required that Olga be back home by 11 o'clock at the latest. ¶ One night Olga didn't return until 2 a.m. Her mistress was furious. When Olga appeared she cross-examined her relentlessly: ¶ "With whom have you been?" she demanded. ¶ "A vent vid Mr. Olson," said Olga demurely. ¶ "Where did you go with him?" ¶ "Ve vent to a movie." ¶ "What did you do then?" ¶ "Mr. Olson he vanted to take a valk." ¶ "Where did you walk to?" ¶ "Ve valked to da park." ¶ "What did you do then?" ¶ "Ve sat on a bench." ¶ "What did you do then?" ¶ "Mr. Olson he kissed me." ¶ "What! You permitted him to kiss you? What happened then?" ¶ "Mr. Olson he fucked me." ¶ "Olga!" A moment's silence. Then the mistress's voice resumed, in a sepulchral tone: "What did you do? What did you say?" ¶ "A said 'Tank you, Mr. Olson.' "

·346·

"Mama," asked the little girl, "does everybody wave their legs in the air when they go to heaven?" ¶ "No, dear, of course not. Where did you get such an idea?" ¶ "Well, just now in the bedroom the maid was waving her legs in the air, and she kept saying 'Oh God, I'm coming! Oh God, I'm coming!' But papa wouldn't let her. He was on top of her and kept holding her down."

·347·

The worst insult a woman can offer a man, in three words of two letters each: ¶ "Is it in?"

·348·

"I want a quiet room," said the guest as he registered. "I've been travelling a long time in a day coach, and I want a good sleep." ¶ The clerk assured him he would be accommodated, and he was conducted to a comfortable room. In a few minutes he was sleeping peacefully, but before long he was wakened by a terrific din. There was shouting and the sound of tin horns and prancing feet and a general hullabaloo. He seized the telephone. ¶ "I told you I wanted a quiet room," he expostulated. "What do you mean, putting me where I can hear such a din?" ¶ "I'm very sorry, sir," said the clerk. "I forgot. You see, they're holding a fireman's ball." ¶ "Well, tell 'em to let go," yelled the guest.

·349·

Yates was telling his wife about his new stenographer. ¶ "She's the most efficient stenographer and typist I ever had," he said. "And she's got style, too. She looks just like a French doll." ¶ Little daughter had been listening. She spoke up: ¶ "Papa, does she shut her eyes when you lay her down on her back, like my doll?"

·350·

The rector and the curate were discussing the abstinences to which they should subject themselves during Lent. They agreed it was proper for each to give up whatever indulgence he liked best. ¶ "That would mean," said the rector, a bachelor, "I'd have to give up my pipe." ¶ "And it would mean," said the curate, "I'd have to give up having intercourse with my wife." ¶ "Well," said the rector, "I'll give up smoking if you'll give up copulation. Is it a bargain?" ¶ "All right," said the curate, without enthusiasm. ¶ A couple of weeks later the curate was awakened by his wife very early one morning. ¶ "William, William!" she whispered excitedly into his ear. "The rector's in the garden smoking!"

·351·

Jones' wife was out of town on an extended visit, and Jones, at the club, was relating an experience he had had the night before with the Juno-like maid who had been left in charge of the house. ¶ "Fellows," he said, "believe it or not, I was just dropping to sleep when my bedroom door opened softly. In she came, without making a sound, in her bare feet. Just as quietly and quickly she slipped into bed beside me. God! You can imagine how I felt." ¶ "How you felt *her*," one of the boys corrected. Jones went on without noticing the interruption: ¶ "She snuggled up to me, pressed her warm soft breasts against me, slipped her leg between mine, crushed me in her arms, and kissed me—Lord! how she kissed me!" ¶ The group by this time was silent, awaiting the *denouement*. But Jones seemed to have become speechless. ¶ "And then— and then what did you do?" someone asked finally. ¶ Jones shook his head slowly. "Do," he repeated. "What could I do? My wife and I love each other. I sent the girl back to her own room. What would you have done?" ¶ "If you ask me," said the fellow sitting next to him, "I'd have done exactly what you did, you lying son-of-a-bitch!"

·352·

A man was crossing the main waiting room of the Grand Central station, carrying a beautiful baby in each arm. As he approached the train gate an elderly woman bustled up and googled over the babies. ¶ "What lovely children," she cried. "What are their names?" ¶ "I don't know," responded the man. ¶ "Are they boys or girls?" ¶ "I don't know, madam," he replied icily. ¶ "Do you mean to say that you are carrying two such lovely children and you don't know their names, or even whether they are boys or girls?" ¶ "Exactly that, madam. These are not my children. I'm a condrum salesman and these are two complaints I'm taking back to the factory."

·353·

Another youngster was in the habit of pissing on the streets, a habit of which his mother wished to break him. She called him and chastised him severely, telling him that if he continued she would be forced to cut his prick off. ¶ "Aw," said he, "what the hell do I care! All the girls have theirs cut off and tucked in."

·354·

May, an actress, was travelling on a train, reading a current copy of a magazine. The gentleman sitting opposite soon engaged her in conversation. They hit it off pretty well. ¶ Just then they passed a field in which a bull was in the act of mounting a cow. May asked him how an animal knew when its mate was in the mood for this kind of skirmish. "Why." he explained, "when a cow or any female animal is in heat she throws off a peculiar odor that is significant to the male." ¶ "Does this apply to humans?" asked May. ¶ "Certainly," responded her companion. ¶ The sight created a warm glow in May and for the rest of the trip she gave him all the sex appeal of which she was capable, with no response from the stranger. When their train arrived at the depot they shook hands and the stranger gave May a card and asked her to phone him sometime. She looked at it and saw that he was a Doctor. She presented him with her card, and this parting crack. "Say Doc, come up and see me sometime, when you lose the cold in your head."

·355·

A woman stepped to the teller's window and presented a twenty dollar gold piece for deposit. The teller remarked, "So you've been hoarding eh?" ¶ "Never mind how I got it." was her snappy reply.

·356·

A salad recipe:
A little chicken, a little pepper, no dressing, and lettuce.

The lady invited him upstairs.

·357·

A young girl facing her first confinement was rather anxious about the details of the parturition period, and asked her doctor question after question. Finally: ¶ "But doctor, what position will I have to lie in when the baby is coming out?" ¶ "Oh, the same position you laid in when you started the kid." ¶ "Oh my God!" she gasped, horrified, "do you mean I've got to drive around Central Park for two hours with my feet hanging out of the window?!"

·358·

A young chorus girl was picked up by a fast worker the other day and ushered into a taxi. ¶ "Let's go up to my apartment and fuck," he said shortly. ¶ With her eyebrows lifting way up to here, she ejaculated: "What? No buildup?"

·359·

A woman walked into the corset department of a New York store and asked to see some maternity corsets. ¶ "What bust?" asked the pert saleswoman. ¶ "A condrum, of course, you fool!"

·360·

Definition of rape: The wrong man.

·361·

A small boy was playing at the curb. A lady in a window looked down very much interested in his game. He had an exceptionally long cock for his age. He would place a pebble on it, strain it back some distance then let the pebble fly into the air. ¶ The lady liked the size of the boy's tool and invited him upstairs. She took him to bed and inserted the prick in her cunt, then gave him a few coins and the boy returned to the street. ¶ After a while she again felt the desire and called to him again. He looked up much annoyed and yelled, "Aw go to hell, you busted my bean shooter."

·362·

Alphonse, after setting up the boys and girls at the cafe to several rounds of toasts in beer and Tom Collinses, wandered home with a bladder full of piss. Passing a little thicket of bushes, he saw his chance to rid himself of a bellyful of piss unobserved. ¶ Just as he pulled his old joy-prong out, however, he became aware of a squatting bimbo near his elbow who was preparing to do the same thing. He would have withdrawn in gallant modesty, but the clear amber fluid was already gushing forth and all the politeness in the world would not restrain it. His companion, who had been a guest at the same bout, was more or less in a similar fix, and was her face red!! She groped for a line of nonchalance: ¶ "Here's to you!" she faltered, carrying the metaphor back to their bacchanal. ¶ "And to you!" he answered, catching on. Then, thinking to improve his opportunity: "But suppose . . . we clink 'glasses'!"

·363·

A musical comedy producer was looking over a group of prospective chorines. He had each one strip, the better to gauge their charms. As the first applicant stood before him he noticed the impression of the letter "H" on her abdomen. ¶ "What's that?" he demanded. ¶ "Well, you see," explained the girl, "my sweetheart's a college man, and he was wearing his college belt." ¶ The next nude girl who presented herself had the letter "Y" similarly impressed on her belly. ¶ "And that means what?" asked the producer. ¶ "Oh, my sweetheart's a collegian and he forgot to remove his belt," responded the applicant. ¶ The abdomen of the next girl showed, in larger letters "F.C." ¶ "I suppose," remarked the producer, "your boy friend's a Fordam College man?" ¶ "No," she said languidly. "He's a Fire Chief, and he forgot to remove his hat."

·364·

"Just 'xactly what is a fairy?" queried the little kindergarten pupil. ¶ "A fairy," answered the absent-minded but up-to-date teacher, "is a pansy with a long stem."

·365·

"Mrs. O'Brien," said her neighbor Mrs. Swartz, "I knocked at your door last night, but you didn't answer. I know you were home because I saw a light under your door." ¶ "Sure I wuz home," said Mrs. O'Brien, "but I wuz busy." ¶ "Busy?" said Mrs. Swartz. "Was you too busy to answer the knock of a friend?" ¶ "That I wuz," replied Mrs. O'Brien. "The baby was suckin', the old man wuz fuckin', and I wuz readin' a book."

·366·

Oscar was the biggest boy in school—bigger, in fact, than his pretty young teacher. But that fact didn't prevent her from keeping him after school one day when he had been particularly obstreperous. She kept him a long time— a very long time—so long in fact, that his pals who waited for him around the corner became quite apprehensive. Finally he emerged, grinning. ¶ "What did she do to you?" they demanded. ¶ "I don't know what it was," Oscar replied, "but it beats pissing all to hell!"

·367·

The social worker had been there before, so she didn't think it necessary to knock before entering. She saw a man leap from the bed, grab his trousers and bolt through the rear door. ¶ The lady in residence didn't condescend even to move. She lay as she had been on the bed, legs apart, panting. ¶ The social worker, speechless for a moment, finally managed to ejaculate: ¶ "And your husband's hardly been dead a week!" ¶ "Yessir," said the lady. "Henry's dead, not me."

·368·

Winters and his wife were enjoying a little vacation, stopping off for a few days in the various towns they wanted to visit. One evening, as they were walking down the hotel corridor to their room, they heard laughter in a room they were passing. The door was slightly ajar, and they peeped in. At one side of the room a man was standing, nude, his penis sticking out. At the other side a nude girl was tossing doughnuts towards him, trying to "ring" his erect tool. ¶ "Gee, I'll bet that's fun," exclaimed Winters. "Let's try it when we get to our room." ¶ "All right," assented his wife, "but you'll have to get some 'life-savers'!"

·369·

A patient in a lunatic asylum would eat nothing but shit. One day an orderly brought in a big bowl of the steaming delicacy, which the patient would not touch. It remained in front of him for three days but no inducing, coaxing or threatening could make him partake of the meal. He simply sat there with his arms folded and sulked. Finally the head warden was called to the fellow's cell. ¶ "Come now, tell me what is the matter?" he pleaded. "Is it that you are tired of eating shit and wish to change your diet?" ¶ "No, of course not." ¶ "What is the matter then?" ¶ "I don't like the way you're treating me and I'm on a hunger strike. Imagine serving a fellow shit to eat, with a hair in it. See it right on top there?" he said, pointing to the bowl.

·370·

And a gigolo, in case you don't know, is the egg that lays the golden goose.

·371·

"Mrs. Sweeney," shouted a voice down the dumb-waiter shaft. "Is the ice-man coming?" ¶ "Not yet," answered Mrs. Sweeney, "but he's breathing hard."

·372·

A Jewish couple registered at a hotel and were assigned to a room. An hour later loud and frantic cries came from the room. ¶ "Listen! What's that?" whispered the house detective to the room clerk. They strained their ears. It was a woman's voice, shrill and piercing: ¶ "Murder! Fire! Police!" ¶ Together the house detective and the room clerk rushed to the room. The cries were continuing. They put their ears to the door. More plainly now they heard the woman's voice: ¶ "Furder, Meyer, please! Furder, Meyer, please!"

·373·

A recruiting sergeant looked up from his desk to behold what obviously was a woman. ¶ "What do you want here?" demanded the sergeant. ¶ "I'd like to join the army, mister," answered the woman. ¶ The sergeant was nonplussed. He didn't know what to say. After some thought he asked: ¶ "D'ye think you could kill a man?" ¶ The woman simpered. ¶ "Yes, sir, I think I could— but it might take several months."

·374·

A Catholic priest had been considerably augmenting the parish funds by imposing, among others, monetary penances upon feminine members of the faith who confessed to sexual sins. He learned, too, that the male participant in these sins was, in almost all the cases, the same man. He was, therefore, somewhat surprised when one day this man presented himself in the priest's study. The caller came to the point quickly. ¶ "I didn't come here to confess, or to listen to any homily," he declared. "I've found out that you're cashing in, in a big way, on my attentions to your lady communicants. Now my proposition is this: Fifty-fifty, or I move out of your parish!"

·375·

Ronald was before a judge, charged with failing to support his large family properly. He proved, however, that he turned over all of his small wages to his wife. He simply didn't earn enough to buy food and clothing for his numerous offspring. ¶ "I'll discharge you," said the judge, "but you'll have to promise the court that there will be no more additions to your family." ¶ Ronald promised. But a few years later he was before the same judge, on the same charge. ¶ "I understand, from information brought to me," said the judge, "that there have been two more babies in your family since you were in this court before." ¶ "Yessir," said Ronald. ¶ "And I told you you must have no more babies," pursued the judge. "You promised me you wouldn't. You knew you couldn't support them." ¶ "Yessir," said Ronald. "But judge, there's times when I feel like I could support the universe."

·376·

While fucking a beautiful girl, a Chinaman farted all the while. The girl was curious and inquired what caused this continuous wind breaking. ¶ "My pricky have such a good time, my assy shouty Hoolray," was the answer.

·377·

Sister Mary had sinned with a man. Everything was in preparation for a high mass of forgiveness. The other nuns would pray that her soul be saved. When all were assembled, Sister Katherine was no where to be found. After searching through the whole convent, she was finally found in her room packing her few belongings. ¶ "Why, Sister Katherine," asked the sister superior, "Aren't you going to pray for the forgiveness of Sister Mary?" ¶ "I've been in this convent for ten years," said Katherine, "and all it has been is fucking and forgiving, fucking and forgiving. Well, I am tired of forgiving. I'm going out and do a bit of fucking for a change."

·378·

A man went to a doctor with the complaint that he thought he was becoming impotent. "Here are three pills which will cost you ten dollars a piece. I guarantee that each time you take one you will get an erection immediately," said the doctor. ¶ "Thirty dollars is a lot of money in these depression days, doc. If you don't mind I'll try one right here to see if they work." ¶ He swallowed a pill and immediately his prick stood up at attention. "How the hell do I get it down again?" asked the patient. ¶ "Just whistle and see what happens," requested the doctor. ¶ He did and sure enough the prick went back to its normal limp condition. ¶ Overjoyed at the discovery, he paid the doctor the thirty hard earned dollars, and boarded a trolley car for home. He could not bring himself to believe that what had happened was true and swallowed another pill on the trolley. Up jumped his cock and stayed up until the whistle from a traffic cop brought it down. ¶ When he got home he telephoned his favorite chorus girl and made a date for that evening. "This is my celebration night," he said, "We'll go to the Ziegfeld Follies, the Central Park Casino and the Ritz Carlton later. Money is no object with me tonight." ¶ When they arrived at the Ritz he rented the royal suite. While the chorus girl was getting undressed he went into the bath-room and swallowed the remaining pill. He then came out and asked her, "What do you think of this?" ¶ "Whew," she whistled.

·379·

A hooker had seasonal greetings tattooed on her legs. On her left thigh she had the flesh-artist inscribe: "Merry Christmas." On the right thigh, "Happy New Year." When the tattooer was through with his work, she turned to the man, whose breath, during the close proximity required by his work, had blown hotly upon her quiff, and said: ¶ "Come up and see me sometime between the holidays."

·380·

A husband and wife and their 18-year-old daughter, all enthusiastic golfers, were on the links. The husband and father foozled. ¶ "Oh, fuck!" he cried in disgust. ¶ His wife turned upon him in righteous wrath. ¶ "Aren't you ashamed of yourself to use such language before your young daughter?" she burst out. "You ought to apologize to her this minute." ¶ He turned to the daughter. ¶ "I apologize," he said. "But, after all, daughter, you're not a child any more. You must have heard that word spoken before?" ¶ "Yes, of course, father," she replied, "but never in anger."

·381·

A travelling man in a small town hotel felt a sudden call to use the toilet in the middle of the night. He hastened down the hall to the door he thought opened into the toilet. It was locked. In a few minutes he tried again. Again he found it locked. Again he waited, until he could stand it no longer, and a third time went down the hall, only to find the door still locked. The door he had been trying led, not to the toilet, but to a room which that night was occupied by a bridal couple. Inside, the groom had been getting nervous under the repeated interruptions, so when he heard the doorknob turned a third time he shouted gruffly: ¶ "What do you want?" ¶ "You ought to know," came the travelling man's voice from without. "If you ain't using both holes in there, I want one."

·382·

A school teacher in a western town who could never get enough of what Rabelais calls the "game of the beast with two backs" got married. Much to the surprise of her friends she seemed to thrive on her reduced fare. One of them, meeting her on the street, asked if she was happy. ¶ "I never knew," she replied, "that I could be content with so little."

·383·

An American and an Englishman were arguing as to which of the two nationalities had the best news-boys. They made a bet and an American news-boy was sent to England. ¶ When they came over to investigate, they found that the English boy had sold very few of his papers, whereas the American lad had but one paper remaining. "Wuxtra!" he was shouting, "All about the King's castration!" ¶ They inquired what he meant by the King's castration, whereupon he pointed to the head-line which read, 'Last of the King's Balls comes off Tonight.'

·384·

The travelling salesman, trying to sleep in his pullman berth, was considerably annoyed by the bridal couple in the berth opposite. Just as he would be dozing off, he would be aroused by hearing the porter summoned to the nuptial berth, and hearing the young bridegroom say: ¶ "Here's a dollar, porter. Bring us two towels." ¶ On the sixth such occasion the salesman stopped the porter as the latter was dispatched on his errand. ¶ "Here," he shouted, loud enough to be heard the length of the pullman. "Here, porter, here's fifty cents. Bring me one towel."

·385·

A young clergyman had been invited to attend a house-party on the Long Island estate of one of his wealthy parishioners. Irked and more or less disgusted by the hilarity which developed as the evening wore on, he excused himself, went to his room, and fell into a light sleep. He was awakened by a light tap at his door. He sprang up and opened the door, to confront one of the young women whose actions, earlier in the evening, had affronted his sense of decorum. ¶ "Did you want me?" he asked, stiffly. ¶ "No, I didn't want you, but I drew you," she giggled.

·386·

A census-taker, gathering data in the Ozark Mountains of Missouri, came across a tumbledown shack about which were playing more than a dozen children. The father was sitting on the doorstep, puffing at a pipe filled with dried cornsilk. The census man explained his mission, and learned that the family's name was Gibson, and the children numbered fourteen. ¶ "Don't you find it hard to look after so many?" he queried. ¶ "Yep," responded the father, "but I don't reckon we're agoin' to have no more." ¶ "How's that?" asked the census-taker. "Have you found a method of control?" ¶ "A what?" ¶ "A method of birth control?" ¶ "Oh, no—but we think we've found out what's-causin' 'em."

·387·

A young man was engaged in conversation with a middle-aged gentleman whom he had met in the club bar. The elder man had taken a liking to the young fellow, and after awhile produced a flask. ¶ "No thank you," said the young man. "I don't drink." ¶ The elder of the two offered a cigar. ¶ "Thank you, sir," said the young man, "but I don't smoke." ¶ They sat in silence a moment while the middle-aged man regarded his companion. ¶ "I like your principles, young fellow," said the elder finally. "My daughter is on the observation platform. I'd like you to meet her." ¶ "Thank you kindly, sir," was the reply, "but I don't fuck."

·388·

At a duck shooting camp, one of the wealthy Joneses was unable to sleep and spent the night miserably wandering about the shack. In the morning he complained to the guide. ¶ "I'll fix you up to-night," said the guide. "Last week there was a guy down here, a married man, and he couldn't sleep either. I gave him a hairbrush to hold and he slept like a baby."

·389·

A famous Broadway actor, held up in Atlanta on a barnstorming tour of the South, while differences in his contract were being ironed out, amused himself each afternoon by playing bridge in one of the local clubrooms. The actor was greatly annoyed at these sessions, by the presence of an old spindle-shanked retired Methodist minister, who kept kibitzing around the table, making disturbing remarks. Finally he determined to rid himself once and for all of this annoyance, by making an obscene remark. ¶ That afternoon he was dealing the first hand when the old preacher popped in, as per custom, and came to peer over the actor's shoulder. The latter turned, spat on the floor and said: ¶ "You know, that last cunt I lapped was awful salty." ¶ The preacher looked at him sympathetically. ¶ "Young man," he said, with a consoling pat on the shoulder, "they're all salty."

·390·

Mrs. Brown and Mrs. Green being both out-of-town, Brown and Green were getting themselves a stag dinner in Brown's home. The talk came to children. Brown had none, while Green, married ten years, had six. ¶ "Nothing we can do seems to work," said Green ruefully. "We've tried every kind of birth control, but they just keep coming." ¶ "That so?" said Brown. "Well, I'll show you what we use—and I'll bet you won't have any more kids. Come with me." ¶ He led the way into the bedroom, opened a bureau drawer, and stood gaping. ¶ "My God!" he exclaimed. "She's taken it with her!"

·391·

One gay told another that he was out with a lovely, great big sailor. The second gay, was very much perturbed, "Certainly," he said, "You could have invited me over, you know I'm crazy about sea food."

·392·

An infamous writer, having passed from this mortal plane, was somewhat surprised to find himself in heaven, facing Saint Peter. He had not expected such favorable treatment in view of the stories which he had related about himself in his autobiography. ¶ "Didn't you read my autobiography?" he asked Peter. ¶ "Sure," replied that arbiter. "But we decided to give you a break anyway." ¶ "That's fine," responded Frank. ¶ "Is there anything we can do for you, anything you want?" asked Peter. ¶ "Well, I wouldn't mind a little nooky," replied the newly-arrived guest. ¶ "Why, we haven't anything of that sort here," said Peter. "If you're still looking for that type of thing I suppose you might find it in hell." ¶ Frank rushed off to the lower regions, and was received with great warmth by His Satanic Majesty. ¶ "I'm looking for some girls, young girls preferred," said the newcomer. "Got any?" ¶ "Certainly," said the devil, "Come right in here." ¶ He ushered him into a room handsomely decorated with Oriental curtains and fabrics and redolent with aromatic odors. Seated on a bed in the corner were four beautifully-formed maidens. Frank eyed their seductiveness with great anticipation, hurried over, pulled away the loose gown from one, and was horrified to find that, though her figure and breasts were ideal, there was no lower opening whatsoever. It was the same with the others. ¶ "Why," he cried, turning to Satan, "these girls haven't got any cunts!" ¶ The devil grinned. "That's the hell of it," he said.

·393·

The cadets in the cavalry troop of a well-known military school, have a tradition that it is all right to have intercourse with a woman during her menstrual period. They explain this by saying, that a good cavalry man should always wade through the mud and blood to glory.

·394·

His lordship was very sick. One morning one of his tenants passed by and met his lordship's butler. The following conversation ensued: ¶ Tenant:—"Good morning Tyson, and how is his Lordship this morning?" ¶ Tyson:—"Oh, he is feeling much better. You know we have been feeding him through the rectum. This morning we gave him some buttered toast and it would have done your old heart good to see his arse hole fairly snap at it."

·395·

A woman writer was attending a polite Hollywood party, at which a male writer, always the leading spirit in mirth and merriment, was adding to the general pleasure of the guests by goosing them vigorously with his thumb. The woman had just entered into a long and serious conversation about the art of making pictures when the man stole up and intruded his thumb into the circle of her sphincter muscle. She pretended not to have felt the goose. He repeated it with more violence. Quite calmly and without turning around, she remarked: ¶ "William, what a cold nose you have!"

·396·

A trollop was walking along the street and passed over a manhole. One of the workers below saw that she wasn't wearing any underwear, and quickly reached out and inserted his finger in her quiff. "How dare you?" she asked, looking down at the man. ¶ "Lady, if your heart is as soft as your cunt you'll forgive me," he replied. ¶ She paused a moment, smiled and said: "Brother, if your prick is as hard as your finger, come up and see me sometime."

·397·

"Why do you always call your butler 'Piles'?" asked the American. ¶ "Because he is such a bloody ass." answered the Englishman.

"I've programmed this one to chase girls!"

·398·

A girl who was enthusiastic about aviation had a picture of Lindbergh tattooed on her right thigh and one of Amelia Earhart designed on the left. The next evening her fiancé called and when conversation veered to matters of aviation she told him what she had done. He asked if he might see the designs, so she pulled up her skirts to the waist. The fiancé gazed admiringly. ¶ "That's a very good drawing of Lindbergh," he said, "and that's good of Earhart too! But say, that one in the middle is a perfect likeness of Balbo."

·399·

A young woman was very much annoyed by the fact that whenever her fiancé called her pet parrot would begin to repeat bits of profanity and vile language which he had picked up. Finally, fearing that she might have to get rid of the bird, she went to a pet store dealer to ask his advice. He told her that a sure remedy for such a situation was to provide the parrot with a mate. Not having a female parrot in the store, he offered the girl an owl, which he said would answer the purpose just as well. So the girl took the owl home and installed it in the cage with her own bird. ¶ That evening the fiancé called, and he had hardly gotten inside the door when the parrot piped up: ¶ "Somebody's gonna get screwed. Somebody's gonna get screwed." ¶ "Who-o?" cried the owl. "Who-o?" ¶ The parrot glared at her. ¶ "Not you, you flat-faced son-of-a-bitch!" he screamed.

·400·

Lord and Lady Chichester were giving a dinner party. Much to her ladyship's embarrassment his lordship had disappeared. Thinking that perhaps he was ill she proceeded to his bedroom and there found him in bed with the butler. Shocked at what she saw she cried out, "My Lord, the least you could be is on top."

·401·

When hubby arrived from business he was very much surprised at his wife's amorous greeting. "Darling," she said, "to-day is your birthday and I have three surprises for you. I am going to blind-fold you and let you guess what they are." This done, she handed him two packages. He opened the first and felt a beautiful dressing robe. Having undone the second package he found no difficulty in guessing that it contained a pipe. ¶ "Now darling, for the third surprise," said the wife. ¶ Just then the telephone rang. She led him into another room and told him to remain there while she answered it. During the interval, our hero let a terrific fart, the odor of which permeated the surrounding territory. He proceeded to fan away the stink by waving his new dressing robe. ¶ When the wife returned, she removed the blind-fold, and he found himself in the dining room. There sat twenty-two of his best friends ready for the birthday celebration. They were the third surprise.

·402·

A doctor at a medical convention was inquiring about contraceptive devices. He questioned a colleague who practiced in Hollywood. ¶ "How do they get rid of babies in Hollywood?" he wanted to know. ¶ "Spit them out of the windows," was the prompt reply.

·403·

Two poodle dogs stood on a curb stone, amiably conversing. Suddenly one turned to the other and warned the bitch: ¶ "Hey, sit down. Here comes that fox terrier with the cold nose."

·404·

Can you imagine how fish would smell if women didn't swim?

·405·

A southern fellow had been convicted of raping a young girl. The girl, it seemed, was a more than willing participant in the fucking, but she was only sixteen years old. ¶ "In this state, sexual intercourse with any female under the age of eighteen constitutes rape under the law," said the judge sternly. ¶ "But I didn't know that," protested the chap. "I always thought it was sixteen." ¶ "It used to be," said the judge, "but the law has been changed, and the age of consent is now eighteen. Have you anything more to say before I sentence you?" ¶ "Yessir," replied the culprit. "I'd like to ask a favor. I'd like to have you let me go for a week before I go to jail." ¶ "What do you want to do in that week?" demanded the judge. ¶ "I want to visit some relatives all around the county." ¶ "What for?" ¶ "Well, judge, you see I've got a lot of cousins an' other friens' living all aroun' here, an' I want to tell 'em about the new law. They're all workin' under the old rulin'."

·406·

A young man and his sweetheart were visiting the zoo. The young man had been there before, so, before conducting the girl to the monkey house he took the precaution to slip away from her and make a preliminary inspection. He found, as he had feared, that many of the monkeys were fucking. Half an hour later he made another quick trip, alone, to see if the monkeys had finished their amatory activities. They hadn't, so he returned to the girl. By this time she was insisting that they visit the monkeys, but he was able to put her off another half hour. At the end of that time he slipped away a third time, only to find the monkeys still enthusiastically screwing. He turned to the keeper in despair. ¶ "Do you suppose they'd quit if I gave them some peanuts?" he asked. ¶ "I don't know," said the bored keeper. "Would you?"

·407·

A little Jewish boy was required to write an essay on Adolph Hitler. A few minutes after the task had been assigned, his teacher, passing looked over his shoulder. On his paper was written in a firm, bold hand: ¶ "Adolph Hitler is a great man." ¶ Passing his desk again in the middle of the period, she looked again. The same sentence and no more was on the paper. She was puzzled. ¶ Passing a third time, near the end of the period, she looked and saw that no more had been written. ¶ "Abe," she said, "that's fine as far as it goes, but it isn't an essay. Haven't you any more to say?" ¶ "Yeah," Abie replied, "but I don't know how to spell——" and he blew out his lips and made that labial sound known as the Bronx cheer.

·408·

A famous writer, called at a famous cathouse to which he had been referred, in Paris. ¶ "How do you do?" beamed the madam. "Would you like a nice French girl?" ¶ "No," said the man. "I'm fed up with French girls." ¶ "Can I interest Monsieur in a very nice Swedish girl?" ¶ "No," yawned the man. "I'm tired of Swedish girls." ¶ "Perhaps a very nice Russian girl? Very unusual, Monsieur." ¶ "No, thanks," said the man, "I wouldn't be interested. I wonder if you've got a boy?" ¶ "Monsieur!" cried the madam, indignantly. "I shall call a policeman!" ¶ "Oh, don't bother," came back the writer. "Really, I'm tired of policemen too."

·409·

Jimmy, a city boy, had spent his first vacation in the country, where, among other unaccustomed sights, he had seen cows milked. The day of his return to town the family had seated themselves about the supper table and his mother started pouring a glass of milk. ¶ "Don't drink that, mother!" Jimmy shouted. "The cow pissed it!"

·410·

A young man from the sticks entered a city hotel, accompanied by a girl he had picked up on the street. The hotel had been recommended to him by the lady in question. As he picked up the pen to register, his unsophisticated eye noted that the page was filled with such names as "John Smith and wife," "James Brown and wife," and so on. He hesitated, as if debating whether to affix a similar signature, when the porter stepped up reassuringly. ¶ "That's all right, sir," he said. "Go right ahead an' sign yourself like the rest. They're all fucktitious names."

·411·

A middle-aged, overfed American, following a night spent making the rounds of the Paris peep-hole shows known as "circuses," felt one of the impulses which, for some years, he had known all too infrequently. He had his guide arrange for him to meet one of the female performers in a private room. But when he found himself actually in the presence of the naked and willing woman, his penis refused to assert its masculine dignity. It had become limp again—hopelessly limp. The lady, however, was not discouraged. Having encountered such situations before, she took the flaccid member in her hands, stroked it, caressed it, rolled it cunningly between her palms, squeezed it, and finally, as a last resort, applied her tongue skillfully to it. All to no avail. At last she gave up. ¶ "I may have been in the circus," she snapped, "but I'm no snake charmer!"

·412·

An old engraver working on a "leg" photo of a movie star for a rotogravure section, looked admiringly at the star's seductive limbs for a long time and then remarked: ¶ "Any son-of-a-bitch that wouldn't center-field on this dame is a God-damned degenerate!" ¶ He smacked his lips.

·413·

A woman passenger on a train of the notoriously slow Erie Railway, gave birth to a baby. When it was all over, and the mother was resting easily, the conductor could no longer conceal his annoyance. ¶ "Madam," he said severely, "you should have known better than to get on a train in that condition." ¶ "Fair enough," the mother responded, "but I wasn't in that condition when I boarded the train."

·414·

Silas, in town from the farm to sell a load of hay, called upon the family doctor and informed the latter he was soon to be married. He wanted some instruction, as he was entirely inexperienced. The doctor asked him if he had a calf. ¶ "Nope," said Silas. ¶ "Any of your neighbors got a calf?" asked the physician. ¶ "Wall, yaas," replied the young farmer. "Neighbor Perkins across the way's got a calf." ¶ "Is it weaned?" ¶ "Not yet, but it's just about time." ¶ "Borrow it," instructed the doctor, "and when you come to wean it, instead of dipping your finger in milk for it to suck, give it your penis. You'll soon get the idea. Then when you come to get married you'll be all set." ¶ A few months later the doctor met Silas on the street. ¶ "Well," said the man of medicine, "I suppose you're all happily married and settled down?" ¶ "Nope," said Silas. "I bought the calf."

·415·

Father and son were watching the usual and unceasing fornications in the monkey house. ¶ "What are they doing, dad?" asked the little boy. ¶ "Why, they're making baby monkeys." ¶ "How long does it take to make a baby monkey?" ¶ "About six months, son." ¶ "Well then, dad, what's their hurry?"

·416·

A young man entered a sporting house and was astonished to encounter his supposedly respectable uncle. The young fellow did some fast thinking and, looking accusingly at his abashed relative, he exclaimed: ¶ "Uncle—of all people in the world! What are you doing in a place like this?" ¶ But the uncle by this time had collected his wits. He replied: ¶ "Assuming that it's any of your damn business—which it isn't—I'm here because I prefer the simulated enthusiasm of a paid prostitute to the dignified acquiescence of your Aunt Clara."

·417·

Q: What did the blind man say when he passed the fish market?

A: "Afternoon, ladies."

·418·

The one-ring circus was pulling up stakes preparatory to moving on to the next town, when the elephant was found to be missing. The circus people enlisted the aid of the local officials, but for hours no trace of the animal was found. Shortly before day-break the phone rang in the sheriff's office. ¶ "This is Mrs. Pendleton—the widow Pendleton," came a shrill excited voice. "I want you to send a lot of men out to my place right away! There's a terrible big animal walking around my orchard." ¶ "What kind of an animal?" ¶ "It ain't quite light enough to see." ¶ "What's he doing?" continued the sheriff. ¶ "He's—he's picking apples with his tail!" ¶ "Picking apples with his tail? What's he doing with the apples?" ¶ "Oh, sheriff! It's just too awful. I—I simply can't tell you what he's doing with them!"

·419·

Friends of Uncle Jason had tried for years, but unsuccessfully, to persuade him to leave the farm long enough for a visit to New York. In vain they painted the glories of the metropolis, even its lures and attractive sins. They couldn't interest him. One day a neighbor who had spent a week in New York was regaling him with tales of Broadway and the Forties. ¶ "And do you know," he continued, "if you stand at Fifth Avenue and Forty-second street you can see a naked woman riding on a white horse!" ¶ For the first time Uncle Jason pricked up his ears. ¶ "Honest?" he asked. ¶ "Honest Injun!" ¶ "By gum, I got a mind to go! I ain't seen a white horse in twenty years!"

·420·

He was a Scotchman, and most of the time he thought far more of a dollar than of a fuck. His frugality in this respect was abetted by the fact that the few joy factories in his city had to pay high for police protection, and the fees were correspondingly high. But the time came—as such times do—when he couldn't stand it any longer. He hied himself to a sporting house, picked out a girl, and accompanied her to her room. ¶ "How much?" he asked, before starting to undress. ¶ "Fifty dollars," said she. ¶ "I wo'ont pay ut," he said. ¶ "I'm sorry," said the girl. "That's the price." ¶ "I wo'ont pay ut," repeated the Scotchman. ¶ "Then we'll go downstairs again," said the girl. ¶ But by this time the Scotchman had had a visual close-up of her charms. He hesitated, and was lost. "Very we'el," he said. He began stripping off his garments and throwing them out of the window. ¶ "Say, are you crazy? What are you doing that for?" asked the girl. ¶ The garments kept sailing through the window. ¶ "When I get thrrough with you," he said, "the styles will have changed."

·421·

Helen was the modern child of modern parents, and she had been given modern instruction in the biological sciences as applied to reproduction. Her parents took her to the wedding of a relative. She sat quietly through the rather brief congregational ceremony. At the end, she asked: ¶ "Is that all?" ¶ "Yes, dear." ¶ "Then why doesn't Henry sprinkle the pollen on her?"

·422·

"Doctor," asked a young married woman, "you've simply got to tell me some method of birth control." ¶ "Why, of course," said the doctor. "I can tell you a very simple and sure way. Just drink a tall glass of orange juice." ¶ "Before, during, or after?" ¶ "Neither. Instead."

·423·

A rich broker occupying a front seat at a Broadway revue, was accompanied by a friend who knew his White Lights. The broker got hot and bothered about one of the girls. ¶ "Find out what she will cost me," he said to his friend. "I want her, and damn the expense!" ¶ A few days later the friend reported. ¶ "I've talked with the girl," he said. "She wants a Park Avenue apartment, a Long Island estate, a Rolls Royce, and six inches." ¶ "You tell the bitch to go to hell," barked the broker. "I won't cut off two inches for the hottest baby that ever fucked!"

·424·

The gal who was so dumb that she thought the soldier's bonus was something she had been getting right along.

·425·

This particular travelling salesman had long been a patron of a certain hotel in a small town, and a friend of the proprietor. So he was more than outraged—he felt a sense of personal insult—when, one day as he was about to enter the hostelry, a freshly-used condrum grazed his ear and plopped on the sidewalk. Bursting with anger, he stalked up to the desk. ¶ "Who's in that room above the door?" he demanded. ¶ The proprietor naturally resented his tone. ¶ "That, sir, is none of your business," he retorted. "Look here," said the salesman, "I've got a reason for wanting to know who's in that room." ¶ "Well, it's none of your business, but since you seem so interested, there's no one in that room but my daughter and my prospective son-in-law." ¶ "All right," said the salesman. "Now you come out to the sidewalk and I'll show you your prospective grandson!"

·426·

A husband came home unexpectedly, to find his wife lying in bed naked and legs astride. A gentleman was just in the act of removing his pants. "What is the meaning of this?" said the irate husband to the stranger. ¶ The stranger, completely ignoring the husband pointed his finger to the woman threateningly, and said, "Madam, if you do not pay your gas bill, I shall shit on the floor with no further ado."

·427·

The gal who swallowed a pin when young didn't feel a prick until she was eighteen.

·428·

Husband and wife were dressing for the opera, when she noticed a button missing from the fly of his trousers. ¶ "You can't go that way," she said. ¶ "Sew it on, then," he replied. But she was so tightly harnessed and corseted that she was unable to bend over to do the sewing. Then she had an idea. ¶ "Go down to Mrs. Corliss in the apartment below. She's clever with the needle, and she'll sew it on in a jiffy," said the wife. ¶ He was gone a long time, and when he did reappear his face was bruised and one eye was blacked. ¶ "Everything was all right," he explained, " 'till she had it all sewed on and leaned over to bite the thread. Just then her husband came in."

·429·

A prissy colonel of engineers who was always bussing the buttocks of his superior officers in hope of advancement, was invited to attend a dinner given by the general in charge of his brigade. Knowing that the general, a gay dog, liked a naughty story, the colonel sought out his sergeant-major. ¶ "Sergeant," he said, "I'm attending a dinner given by General Dumbguard. Do you know any naughty stories I could tell the general?" ¶ "I know a conundrum," said the sergeant-major. ¶ "What is it?" ¶ "Why is my small arm like a thermometer?" ¶ "Why is your penis like a thermometer?" ¶ "Because it rises when it gets hot." ¶ "Good," said the colonel, and that night he asked the same conundrum at the general's dinner party. ¶ The officers puzzled over it for a long time, and then a second-lieutenant at the foot of the table rose and said: ¶ "I think I know why Colonel Stupidsentry's pigglepozer is like a thermometer." ¶ "Why?" asked the general. ¶ "Because it's full of mercury," said the lieutenant.

When he did reappear, one eye was blacked.

·430·

A patient asked his doctor to try to do something for his voice, which was high and squeaky. The doctor finally agreed to it, but said an operation would be necessary. A couple of weeks after the operation the patient came back and said, "Doctor, oh doctor, my voice is still too high. Can't you make it lower?" ¶ So the doctor operated again. Two weeks more passed and the patient returned. "Doctor," said he, in a bull-frog bass, "My God, can't you do something about this? This is awful." ¶ The doctor scratched his head, and finally called to his nurse. "Oh, Miss Jones," he said, "bring me in that bottle labeled John Smith." ¶ A moment's pause, and then Miss Jones, from the next room, in a rich baritone, "Why, doctor, you don't mean that bottle that had the two olives in it, do you?"

·431·

Boy to cock-teaser he has taken out, and finally given up, "Thanks for the ostrich party." ¶ Cock-teaser: "Ostrich party?" ¶ Boy: "Yes: all neck and no tail."

·432·

Absent minded dentist to virgin bride "Now open a little wider, please."

·433·

While riding on a train out west, a New England school teacher saw what she thought looked like an authentic Indian. She walked up to him and said, "Pardon my seeming familiarity, but are you an Indian?" ¶ "Uh, Uh," he answered. ¶ "How many wives do you have?" ¶ "Gottem eight wives." ¶ "What do you do with so many wives?" ¶ "Me fuckum." ¶ "Why! you dog." ¶ "Me fuckum dog too!" ¶ "But my dear." ¶ "Me no can fuckum deer, deer run too fast."

·434·

There was a farmer chopping down a tree in his backyard. He had hardly struck the axe into the bark than the queen of the fairies put her head out from a hollow in the bole of the tree and pleaded with him. ¶ "Farmer, spare this tree. It intimately lives with rain and provides a home for a lot of fairies. If you spare it I will give you three wishes and I will grant them no matter what they are." ¶ The farmer, overjoyed, threw away his axe and went home to his wife. He told her what had passed between him and the kind fairy. The wife wept with joy. ¶ Cranking up their Model T Ford they drove into town, parked their car and walked up and down Main Street trying to see something that they might want. ¶ Before the windows of Woolworth's Five-and-Ten they paused and looked at a mechanical egg beater. The wife admired the gadget. ¶ "I wish I had one like that." ¶ Immediately it was in her hand. ¶ Her husband was furious. ¶ "To think that you could have wished for a steam yacht, an ermine wrap or a million dollars and all you did was waste your wish on a five-and-ten cent egg beater. I wish you had it jammed up your ass." ¶ He used his third wish getting it out of his wife's bung-hole and they lived contentedly ever after.

·435·

A big star, 'tis said, used to boast he could make any girl in his show—and had. On one occasion, he was bragging that he'd taken out every dame in his current production. "Yeah?" said his listeners. ¶ "Yes," said the star, "and look, what's more, I laid them all too." ¶ "Yeah?" ¶ "Yeah, and look, what's more, that ain't all, I satisfied them, too." ¶ "Yeah, you big mouth!"

·436·
THE TRANSYLVANIA SCREW SONG

Tune: "The Red and the Blue"

Come all you loyal bastards now, you sons-of-bitches
    too,
And lift your farts and cunt-rags for the royal fuck and
    screw.
Old Harvard has her pansies, Cornell her P.I.'s too,
But for old Transylvania we'll screw and screw and
    screw.
Chorus:
Whore whore! Whore whore! Transylva-ni-aw
Whore whore for the fu-uck and the screw
Whore whore! Whore whore! Whore whore!
    Whore whore
Whore whore for the fu-uck and the screw.

·437·

We are from Ivy Hall, from Ivy Hall are we
We never lose our virginity.
For every evening when we go to bed
We raise the sheets up over our head
There is no scandal, for we use a candle
Hurrah girls for Old Ivy Hall
Balls
    Balls
        Balls

·438·

There was a young man from Toluse
Who thought he would bugger a goose
But the sagacious bird
Stuffed her ass with a turd
He decided it wasn't no use.

·439·

Army Mess Song:
They say we get milk in our coffee
They say we get milk in our tea
They say we get milk on our oatmeal
But it tastes like saltpetre to me
Chorus:
Bring back, bring back, oh bring back my manhood to
me, to me
Bring back, bring back, oh bring back my manhood to
me.

·440·

A sweet young strip dancer named Jane
Wore five inches of thin cellophane
When asked why she wore it
She said, "I abhor it
But my cunt juice would spatter like rain."

·441·

There was a young man from Leith
Who stripped long cocks with his teeth.
It was not for mere pleasure
He adopted this measure
But to get all the cheese underneath.

·442·

There was a young fellow named Tucker
Who, instructing a novice cock-sucker,
Said, "Don't bow out your lips
Like an elephant's hips
The boys like it best when they pucker."

·443·

There was a young saphic named Anna
Who'd stuff her pal's cunt with a banana,
Then she'd eat bit by bit
From her partner's warm slit
In the most approved lesbian manna.

·444·

There was a young man from the coast
Who ate melted shit on his toast
When the toast saw the shit
It collapsed in a fit
For the shit was it's grandfather's ghost.

·445·

There was a young fellow called Skinner
Who took a young woman to dinner
They started to dine
At half after nine
And at quarter of ten he was in 'er.

·446·

There was a young priest of Dundee
Who went back of the parish to pee
He said Pax Vobiscum
Why the hell don't the piss come
I must have a D-O-S-E.

·447·

Having consulted some of the finest doctors in this
country to no avail, he finally went to the most eminent
physician in Germany, who could tell him no more about
his ailment than the doctors at home. Being very interested
in the case, the doctor did, however, give him a letter of
introduction to a specialist with whom he had attended

college and who had risen to great heights in the medical profession, before he went half insane and retired. ¶ The German doctor knew that if anyone in the world could tell this fellow what ailed him, it was his friend Doctor S. . . . , and, consequently took a chance in sending his patient there, for everyone in the medical profession knew of Doctor S. . . .'s terrible temper; knew that he had thrown out bodily any number of patients who had had the courage to try to get his opinion of their ailments. ¶ Being warned of these things, the chap went to Paris and proceeded to find the address of this mad genius of a doctor, who was the last hope and only remaining chance of finding out what ailed him. ¶ After much trouble, for the street was not listed in the Paris directory and very few people had ever heard the name before, he came to what was more a winding alley than a street, and to the dirtiest alley he had ever seen before. Huge rats boldly ate human shit in the middle of the passageway; and if a pedestrian did not step carefully around the beasts, the chances were that he would be similarly attacked. ¶ As he walked, looking for the number of the doctor's house and stepping carefully over dead cats that were being devoured with equal speed by ragged urchins and millions of swarming flies, while dodging many a turd emitted from the ass-holes that were sticking out of the glassless windows, he was happy inside, and had not the many years of intense suffering completely taken from him the art of smiling, he may have smiled to himself at the thought that at last he would find an answer to the riddle that had caused all this misery in his existence. ¶ Finally, becoming exasperated by the absence of numbers on the tumble-down dwellings, he interrupted a small boy from jerking off, and asked to be directed to Doctor S. . . .'s house. ¶ After calling him an ass-hole sucker and cunt lapper for interfering with his sport, the boy said that he knew where the doctor lived, and would gladly take him there if he would first suck his cock for compensation. Though he had never sucked a cock before, and this boy's was extremely cheesy, he did not wish to be frustrated after having gotten this far in his errand, and went down on the youngster, much to the amusement of the other children, who paused from their various activities to see such a rare sight as the well-dressed stranger sucking-oc Francois the Syphilitic, as they playfully called him, because both his parents had died from that disease. Francois then directed him to the doctor's house, which was a little more tumble down than the rest, and left him by saying, "There, you dirty cock-sucker, I hope the old prick cuts your balls off, the way he did my father's, and eats them for supper." ¶ Groping his way through all kinds of shit in the dark hallway, he finally came to the doctor's door and knocked timidly at first, but when there was no answer he banged with both fists until his knuckles bled, having been warned that the doctor was deaf. ¶ After some time the door was opened a slight crack and a pair of eyes that looked like irridescent, rotting meat, peered through the opening. Next came a beard that was a solid mat of hair held together by the drippings of many years food, spits of tobacco, vomit and what looked suspiciously like consumptive blood. Over the beard were what had once been lips, but were now pieces of raw, hanging flesh, which the now toothless gums chewed incessantly. ¶ Too horrified to speak by the sight that confronted him, the stranger stood in a cold sweat, his knees trembling, not knowing whether to run, or rather, not having the power to. ¶ He had been standing there what seemed an eternity, when suddenly the thing beyond the now half open door asked, "Well, what the fucking hell do you want here?" The voice was more the bark of a mad dog than that of a human being, and the hot breath reeking of a most inhuman and sickening stink hovered about the nostrils of the stranger for what seemed another eternity. At last he answered and handed the doctor the letter of introduction,

which he read, spit in, crumpled up and threw on the
floor at the stranger's feet. He then stared at him, looked
him over from head to foot and said. "Alright, you god
damned pimp, come in and I'll look you over. But only
as a special favor to my old friend Doctor H. . . . . . ."
"He was the first man whose ass-hole I ever sucked."
He mused, shaking his head in glee as he led the way
through heaps of tin cans and garbage into the consulting
room, as he jokingly called the hovel they entered. ¶ "Sit
down." He commanded the stranger, who sat on the
frame of what had once been a chair, causing bed bugs
and cockroaches to scurry. ¶ "Well, I have no time to
waste on shitheels like you, let me see some of your
spit." ¶ The stranger looked around helplessly for a receptacle in which to spit, but the doctor cupped his hands
and said, "here, spit here." ¶ The doctor looked at the
spit, smelled it, tasted it, and wiped his hands on the
gray, wire like, hairs of his head. ¶ "Nothing wrong with
that." said he. "Let me see your piss." ¶ Again he
cupped his hands, wherein the stranger pissed. ¶ "Nothing
wrong with that." said the doctor, after smelling, tasting
it and wiping his hands on his beard. ¶ "Let's have a
look at your shit." he commanded. ¶ He followed the
same procedure with the shit as he had with the spit and
piss. At this point, the stranger became too nauseated to
stand it any longer and vomited. Instantly the doctor was
in front of him with cupped hands, catching as much of
the green and yellow liquid as he could hold. He brought
his hands to his mouth with a quick movement, rolled
the vomit around on his tongue, much in the manner of
a wine connoisseur, and with a glint of joy in his irridescent
eyes said, "The trouble with you young fellow, is that
you have a weak stomach."

·448·

A child of fifteen, a beautiful young girl, had been
invited to a sorority dance, her first. Her mother, well

aware of the younger generation's pranks and fancies, called the child to her and said: "You wouldn't want to bring disgrace on your mother, would you?" ¶ "Oh, no, mother," the beautiful child replied. ¶ "Then listen to me. When you go to the sorority dance I don't want you to let any boy hold your hand. That would bring disgrace to your mother, and you wouldn't want to do that." ¶ "I'll do as you say, mother," the girl agreed. ¶ "Another thing," said the mother. "Don't let any of the boys kiss you. If you let them, that would bring disgrace upon your mother." ¶ "I understand, mother, "said the girl. ¶ "Wait, there's still another thing I must tell you. Under no circumstances let any of the boys get on top of you, darling. If you did, that would bring disgrace upon me. And you wouldn't want to do that, would you?" ¶ "Of course not, mother." ¶ It was much after midnight when the beautiful little girl returned home. Her mother had not yet been able to fall asleep, but lay in bed, reading. ¶ "Well, darling," she greeted her daughter, "did you have a good time?" ¶ "Oh, yes, mother." ¶ A little frown creased the mother's brow. ¶ "Tell me," she said. "Did you let any of the boys hold your hand?" ¶ The child hesitated for a moment. Then, hesitantly: "Yes, mother, but only one of them: Johnny Smith." ¶ "Don't you know you were bringing shame and disgrace on me?" the mother asked. ¶ The beautiful little girl bowed her head. ¶ "Did any of the boys try to kiss you?" the mother demanded. ¶ Again the girl hesitated. ¶ "Yes, mother, she admitted. "Johnny Smith kissed me." ¶ "That's terrible," the mother cried. "You might have remembered that he was disgracing and shaming me." ¶ "I'm sorry, dear." ¶ "One more question," the mother said. "Did you let Johnny Smith get on top of you?" ¶ "Oh, no, mother," the girl cried quickly, smilingly, "I wouldn't let him bring disgrace to you. I wouldn't bring shame to you. Only Johnny's mother will be disgraced. *I got on top of him!*"

"Oh, yes, mother!"

·449·

A famous New York author whose common-sense takes strange forms, at times tells a story to prove that it is always cheaper to take a cab than to ride in the subway. Planning a trip to Brighton Beach, his economical wife suggested they take the B.M.T. and overrode his objections that a cab would be more economical in the long run. In new summer clothes and with their bathing suits they set out. They were seated peacefully, thinking of nothing in particular and looking at nothing but the advertisements across the way when suddenly something flashed past the author's nose and lit on the lapel of his light grey suit. He looked. It was a blob of shit. He looked up. Hanging to a strap was a girl in a white summer frock, trembling with fear and nervousness. At her feet was a puddle of liquid shit. It had spread until it touched the lunch boxes placed between the feet of the passengers and they were engaged in wiping off their lunch boxes on the girl's dress. A fight started and they began to toss the shit around at each other. It was thrown from one end of the car to the other. The author and his wife were liberally be-sprinkled. ¶ The moral of the story, according to the author, is that it cost him twice as much in cleaning bills as it would have cost to ride all the way to Brighton Beach in a cab.

·450·

A monkey had done a good deed for an elephant, and as compensation the elephant was allowing herself to be screwed by the little fellow. They were doing the dirty work under a cocoanut tree, and one of the cocoanuts fell, hitting the elephant on the head. She let out a fierce bellow that could be heard for miles around, and the monkey asked, "Am I hurting you, honey?"

"Ohhhh, Charlie, you devil, you!"

·451—500·

Pornographic Questionnaire No. 1

QUESTIONS

1. What horse drowned how many people with urine in the city of Paris?

2. Why did the lady use a glass diaphragm?

3. How long was it necessary for the parents of Hercules to copulate before the hero was conceived?

4. Complete the touching ballad beginning: "When the lady first came West—"

5. Who is the world's most perverse, diseased, living man?

6. Give thirty synonyms for the word 'penis' as suggested by Rabelais.

ANSWERS

1. Garagantua's mare drowned six hundred bakers' apprentices when she pissed in the streets of Paris. (See Dore's illustration.)

2. She wanted a womb with a view.

3. Forty-eight hours, and a good job well done, say the editors.

4. "When the lady first came West,
        She taught school,
But now she likes fucking best, etc. to the final denouement, when the loser in the great screwing match, that inimitable whore, despite 'bunt and shunts and double shunts and things unknown to common cunts, dies with her boots on under the incessant prodding of the cowboy's great peter.

5. Adolph Hitler: He fucked his way into power; browned all the German youth; fucked the Jews out of their possessions; clap-ped them in jail; syph-ted the literature of the country; has the scum of Germany behind him and now he wants to lick the hole of France.

6. Little dille, staffe of love, quillety, faucetin, dandilollie, peen, jolly kyle, bableret, emebretoon, quickset imp, branch of coral, female adamant, placket-racket, cyprian scepter, jewel for ladies, bunguetee, stopple too, busherusher, gallant wimble, pretty boarer, ney-burrow ferret, little piercer, augretine, dangling hangers, down right to it, stiffe and stout, in and to, pusher, dresser, pouting stick, honey pipe, etc., etc. . . . . .

Pornographic Questionnaire No. 1

7.   In the first paragraph of what famous story occurs the sentence, "The blackmoor dismounted from the Queen's breast."

8.   What . . . . . ?

9.   What fictional character claimed he fucked a hundred times in one night?

10.   Where is Daddy Browning now employed? What are his duties?

11.   List thirteen outstanding works of pornography without which no library is complete.

12.   At what games did Gargantua play while he was a student in Paris? Mention at least three.

ANSWERS

7. The first tale in the *Thousand and One Nights*.

8. . . . .

9. Sir Olivier, the hero of Anatol France's story, "The Boast of Sir Olivier." When Olivier's bride was asked to substantiate the story she confessed to having lost track after the one hundredth seminal shot.

10. Daddy Browning is packing tongues into boxes for a canning company.

11. Fanny Hill, Perfumed Garden, My Secret Life (Eleven Volumes), Marquis De Sade's The Boudoire, Grushenka, Anecdota Americana I and II, Voluptuous Army, Susan Aked, Immortalia, Rosa Fielding, Randiana and Forberg's Manual of Classical Erotology.

12. At seek-and-find, at push-a-little, at odds-and-evens, at the game of love, and at sundry other pastimes, all the while farting and spewing and shitting to the wonder and the amazement of all his professors.

Pornographic Questionnaire No. 1

QUESTIONS

13.   Explain the use of a suspended basket in sophisticated fornication.

14.   What is the height of slipperiness?

15.   What are the meanings of the expressions (a) Eat fur pie (b) "Let it soak" (c) Fornicabubria?

16.   In which work of Shakespeare does the following appear: "The bawdy hand of time strokes hard upon the prick of noon."?

17.   What great poet said: "What is so sweet as sweat after intercourse?"

18.   What is the meaning of the expression 'cold mutton' as used by the poets of the Mermaid Tavern in speaking of wenching parties along the Thames?

ANSWERS

13. It is used to complete the circle of love. A grass basket with a large, smooth-edged hole in the center is suspended by four cords to within ten inches of a bed. The man, on the sofa or bed, drives home from beneath the woman, ensconced in the basket, and then twirls it around, tightening the cords. When released the basket rotates until it achieves its original position. According to its protagonists, this form of sexual relaxation provides the most exquisite pleasure one can obtain in a *corporeal way*.

14. Two eels fucking in a barrel of snot.

15. (a) Otherwise known as "cleaning the kitchen," "Gobbling the gravy," "Getting down on it," scientifically *cunnilingus en vaigna*. (b) "Let it soak," an expression used by dear little whores who drum playfully on your buttocks with their heels just after you have impregnated them with waters from the fountain of life. (c) Fornicabubria is a polite way of saying to screw, to diddle, to hold serious dalliance, to hump, to lay siege with cannon against the bulwarks of maidenhead, etc.

16. Romeo and Juliet.

17. Baudelaire.

18. By it they meant that a woman was either cold, loose as the gates to Gehenna, or afflicted with *frigidis en fallopia*.

Pornographic Questionnaire No. 1

19. Give the lewd version of Christopher Marlowe's death.

20. What people do what, when sodomizing geese?

21. Who was speaking about what when he said, "Let me jump her before she gets cold"?

22. Trace the following quotation:
    "Adultery! Die for adultery? No—
    For Gloucester's bastard son
    Was kinder to his father, than my daughter
    Got 'tween the lawful sheets."

23. Name 10 methods of inducing a sexual orgasm.

24. What is the meaning of the phrase, "listening to the nightingales" and from what noted Italian story-writer's book, is it taken?

ANSWERS

19. Marlowe was taken in coitus by an irate husband and slain; another version claims that the poet's dangler was trapped by muscular contraction and that he was unable to get up from the whore. Her husband slew him, cut off his chief ornament and drew it forth, then lay down in the bed that Christopher had so innocently warmed for him.

20. The Chinese cut off the heads of the geese, that they sodomize, just at the moment of ejaculation.

21. A drunkard to his companions on finding a dead woman in his path; commonly attributed to soldiers of a certain British regiment.

22. King Lear, in Shakespeare's play of that name, condones the "crime" of adultery on the basis that unlicensed screwing leads to better results.

23. By tongue, by hand, by dextrous use of the eye lashes, by tickling with the toes, by manipulating the breasts, by injecting the phallus under the arm pits or into the anus, by the swallowing of filth and ordure, by rubbing against the body of the puella and by a well directed fart.

24. An expression culled from Boccaccio. A decent way of saying that a lady likes her nooky is to say, "She likes to listen to the nightingales."

Pornographic Questionnaire No. 1

25.   What did the five-year old Garagantua find to be the most suitable *torchcul,* or breech-wipe? What other materials, animals and plants did he use in performing this necessary act?

26.   How did the subtle Pantagruel revenge himself upon a lady who would not listen to his right righteous suit?

27.   Who was the first female to claim an "immaculate conception"?

28.   What do tight blue jeans and Brooklyn have in common?

29.   What strange devices do the Mohammedan brides of the Terek Tartars use to convince their husbands of their doubtful virginity?

30.   What is the "French disease" in Italy, and the "Italian disease" in France?

ANSWERS

25.   The neck of a living grey goose. Method: the head held in the left hand, the body passed betwen the legs and the feet held in the right hand, massage gently, paying no heed to honking. Garagantua recommends this as being soothing, soft, gentle and delightful. Other materials which he substituted for *papiere de toilette* were the bed clothes, the curtains, his mother's perfumed gloves, burdock leaves, poison ivy, a wild cat, a fur piece and the tongue of a newly killed goat.

26.   Pantagruel stole the secretion from the vagina of a bitch in heat, and under cover of the matinal prayers managed to rub it on her garments. On the lady's release from church all the dogs of Paris came flocking up to piss on her. (A right suitable revenge; women should not deny themselves to lusty lovers like Pantagruel, whose prick was stiffer than Priam's. V.L.).

27.   The nymph Diane, who claimad to have been impregnated by the seed of Jove, left, oh so carelessly, on a rock adjoining her favorite pool.

28.   Flatbush.

29.   A small fish bladder, filled with beet juice, has the desired effect, a few screams lending proper atmosphere to the setting. According to the Tartars, this simple expedient bambozzles the most keen-witted bridegroom.

30.   Gonorrhea.

Pornographic Questionnaire No. 1

QUESTIONS

31.   Define: (a) fucking (b) passive pederasty (c) schustern (d) buggery.

32.   Describe the mechanics of intercourse between a woman and a horse.

33.   In what celebrated poem does one character fart full into the face of another?

34.   By what arguments did the merchant seduce the nun, whom Casanova befriended, and who later suitably rewarded him?

35.   What do certain women mean when they pervert the verb, 'to kiss'?

36.   To prevent what disease did a foreign government legislate to make it compulsory for men and women engaged in giving libidinous exhibitions to wear a covering or ''belt''?

37.   Give the first names of the three Merry Widows.

38.   What Biblical character slept with his own daughter?

ANSWERS

31. (a) To enjoy oneself in a proper and fitting manner with puellae. (b) The position taken by a young man when he looks through a port hole in the navy. (c) The Teutonic expression corresponding to (a). (d) Sodomy or pederasty or taking or giving it in the ass.

32. Oat bins are usually provided with curved tops, over which a woman may drape her "form devine" at the right height and angle for the horse's comfort. A pony is best used for this type of work.

33. "The Reeve's Tale" by Chaucer.

34. To obtain genital satisfaction, he told her it was not until the third time a woman held coitus that it was possible for her to become pregnant. That was a white lie.

35. Only that they are fain to suckle a man's staff of life.

36. Syphillis spread from one performer to another in the famous sex-show entertainment, and it was necessary to get out a police order, commanding all performers to wear "safety" caps. Later another edict made it illegal for a man and a woman to give immoral showings of their bedroom arts. So now two women, one armed with a "belt", make a mock and travesty of ye good art of fornicabubria.

37. Agnes, Mabel and Becky. Price: all three for 50 cents at any good drug store.

38. Lot.

Pornographic Questionnaire No. 1

QUESTIONS

39. What woman was in the habit of drowning her lovers after a single night of exquisite delight?

40. Supply the missing word in this quotation: "Thou shalt not lie with the——, for it causeth confusion."

41. What famous Frenchman loved negresses and dwarfed women, and stated that his idea of perfect sexual enjoyment was to kiss the naked soles of beautiful women's feet, the woman to be suspended by her thumbs above his head, devoid of clothing?

42. Who is the world's tallest man?

43. What Queen of the Middle Ages told the smuttiest stories only to point a moral?

44. "I want the clap so that I can give it to the maid; the maid'll give it to momma, and momma'll give it to poppa. That's the guy I want to get." What king of France was the victim of such a vengeance?

45. Describe the ways in which the Brobdingnagian housemaids fondled Gulliver, as narrated in "Gulliver's Travels."

ANSWERS

39. Thamara, during whose copulations 'Strange and passionate music was heard in the murmurous night.'

40. "Thou shalt not lie with the beasts for it causeth confusion."

41. Verlaine.

42. Simpson, the pawn-broker. You can walk under his balls.

43. Margaret of Navarre, authoress of the *Heptameron*.

44. Prince Henry of Navarre was so rewarded for indiscreet conduct with the wife of a physician, who purposely contracted syphillis so as to pass it on to his erring wife. Henry went on a pilgrimage following the vendetta. Louis the Fourteenth in his dotage was served with the same trick, and died from causes following the application of too much mercury. "A moment with Venus and a lifetime with Mercury."

45. The big babies made Gulliver crawl about their huge nipples, and squat with bare buttocks on their tits. Also he was made to explore the depths of their navels and dive deep into their cunts, which he describes as being like huge waterfalls, and slippery withal. The spots and blotches in some of these caverns disgusted the intrepid explorer.

Pornographic Questionnaire No. 1

46. What is the meaning of the following expressions in relation to sexual intercourse: (a) "the Indian way" (b) "the French way" (c) a la mode (d) "shoot the chutes"?

47. What great English poet is responsible for the following lines:
> "Then you and I, Sir Arbutnot,
> May knock up whores alone."

48. What is the height of noise?

49. What rare pornographic autobiography holds the overwhelming record for sexual gratifications obtained in unconventional settings? Name at least twenty-five such.

50. (A) What "esoteric" work contains a description of the superlatively orgiastic grand opening of a fashionable whore house? (B) How were the guests invited? (C) What was the climax of the festivities?

ANSWERS

46. (a) Substitution of ear for vagina. (b) mouth for vagina. (c) coating of shaving soap is spread on the male organ. (d) heads of sexual partners at opposite end of bed.

47. Alexander Pope.

48. Two skeletons fucking on a tin roof.

49. My Secret Life. In an empty house, in water-closets and privies, in cabs, in railway carriages, in a church, in a cemetery, in a cow shed, in a barn, in a loft, in a stable, in a brickyard, in fields, on grass, in streets, on the sea shore, in a bath, on top of a tower, on the floor, on chairs, on a carpenter's bench, against an arm chair, against walls, against fences, against trees, against windows, against a bed, against a kitchen dresser.

50. (A) "Grushenka." (B) Specially engraved and embellished invitations were sent to the noblemen of Moscow who were asked to "sample" the house without charge. (C) The public deflowering of ten virgins by volunteering guests.

Note: Question and Answer number 8 were too indecent to print even in this privately printed questionnaire.

Addenda

·501·

(It is always interesting to observe the changes and perversions which a story undergoes when passed along by word of mouth. Often the very point is lost in the retelling. ¶ After No. 212 was printed, the following version of the same anecdote came to hand. It is so patently the original story, and so great an improvement over the other one that we hereby offer it for your comparison.)

A rather shabbily dressed man, by dint of great persistence and repeated statements that he had a million dollar idea to present, succeeded finally in gaining audience with a famous financier. ¶ "Well, what's your proposition?" asked the latter. "Come to the point, you know I'm a busy man." He glanced at the other's clothing disapprovingly. ¶ "I've got the greatest invention of all time," said the other. "I've discovered a way to make cunt-juice taste like orange juice. All it needs is the proper financial backing, and—" ¶ The next thing the inventor knew he was lying out in the middle of the street. He picked himself up and walked away. ¶ A year later a big limousine was parked outside the famed financier's office and a man dressed in the height of fashion descended. He went up to the money man's office and was promptly admitted. ¶ "Excuse me," said the financier, eager to receive such an obviously important personage. "I don't quite remember—" ¶ "Why, I'm sure you must remember me," said the other. "I've just organized a fruit packing company. Made two millions already. You know, I came to you last year with an idea about making cunt-juice taste like orange juice—" ¶ "What!" cried the financier in amazement. "You don't mean to say you succeeded in putting that over?" ¶ "No," replied the visitor. "After I left you I improved on that. I discovered a process to make orange juice taste like cunt juice, and now we're thirty days behind in shipments."

·502·

(This is a long one, and mild withal, but may be found useful for a sedate parlor recitation.)

One pleasant evening in June two men, Mr. Smith and Mr. Jones, were talking in a well-known hotel, in Chicago. A man rushed past them suddenly, muttering, "Son-of-a-bitch, son-of-a-bitch," and Mr. Smith turned to Mr. Jones and asked, "Jones, have *you* ever been called a son-of-a-bitch?" ¶ "Well," said Jones, "not directly." ¶ "And how in hell," asked Smith, "could you be called a son-of-a-bitch indirectly?" ¶ "It was like this," said Mr. Jones . . . and told the following story: ¶ Mr. Jones was sitting in the lobby of that very same hotel one evening when a beautiful young lady, her arms loaded with packages, passed him. Directly in front of him she dropped one of the packages, and Mr. Jones gallantly picked it up. A moment later she dropped two more packages, and he picked those up. Then, near the door, she dropped the lot, and he picked those up as well. During this time he observed that she was very beautiful indeed, and as he returned the last of her packages, he said, "I really think you should have someone see that you get home safely with all those packages." ¶ She agreed that this might be a good idea, and Mr. Jones escorted her to a taxi. She gave an address on the North Side, and during the drive Mr. Jones managed, in spite of the packages, to hold her hand. When they reached the apartment house where she lived he said, "I really think you need help carrying those bundles up in the elevator," and she agreed with him. ¶ Mr. Jones followed her into the apartment, and he put down the packages and they sat down together on a large divan. Mr. Jones had a flask in his pocket, and before long, one thing leading to another, he found himself admiring the young lady's really beautiful legs and ankles. ¶ "Oh," she said, "there are other things much more beautiful than my legs, but I need to be coaxed before I will show them to you. I am passionate, I need to be inflamed." ¶ "And how," said Mr. Jones, "do I inflame you?" And he leaned nearer. ¶ "Oh, not like that!" called the young lady, pushing him away. "You must take off all your clothes, and I will take off mine, and then you must chase me." ¶ Mr. Jones was not as thin as he once was, and he did not run quickly or well, but in a moment he found himself, minus his clothes, chasing the beautiful young lady around and around her apartment. Her body was even more beautiful than he had imagined, but run as he might, he could not catch her. She kept ahead of him, her white legs twinkling so fast he could hardly see them, calling over her shoulder, "I must be inflamed! I must be inflamed!" ¶ Around and around the dining-room table, through the kitchen and back again, into the living-room and back to the dining-room, Mr. Jones chased the beautiful young lady. He grew pretty warm, panting a good deal, but she kept on running and calling, "I must be inflamed!" ¶ At last she rushed into her bedroom and locked the door. "Now you must break down the door," she called. "I am passionate—I need to be inflamed." ¶ By this time Mr. Jones had grown tired of inflaming, and he decided that breaking down bedroom doors was not his business, no matter how beautiful and passionate the young lady behind the door might be, so he dressed and went home and to bed—alone. ¶ The next evening, at the same time, he was sitting in the lobby of his residence hotel when the beautiful young lady came by, her arms once more loaded with packages. She did not see him, but instead dropped a package in front of a man sitting near him. The man jumped up and gallantly picked up the package. Mr. Jones watched with interest, and when the young lady dropped all her packages near the door,

and the strange man recovered the lot and then escorted
her to a taxi, Mr. Jones decided to go along. So he got
into another taxi, and gave the address of the North Side
apartment house where the young lady with the packages
lived. ¶ When he reached the apartment house, however,
Mr. Jones did not go in the front door. Instead, he went
around the back door and climbed up the fire escape to
the sixth floor, where the young lady lived. The shade
was drawn to within a foot of the bottom, but Mr. Jones
got down on his knees and looked through the aperture.
At first he could see nothing, but before long a pair of
beautiful white legs flashed past, running so fast he could
scarcely see them, and behind them a long pair of legs
covered with a thick growth of curling black hair. The
black hairy legs leaped and ran, but they could not catch
up with the white legs, which flashed back and forth,
around and around, until Mr. Jones was nearly dizzy
watching them. ¶ He sat back on his heels as the legs
passed again, and said, aloud, "Oh, boy, look at that!"
¶ "Yeah," said a voice in his ear, a man's voice—"you
should have seen the son-of-a-bitch who was here last
night!"

·503·

(This limerick is the favorite of its author, who also
happens to be the author of a flock of best sellers. What
a mind!)

> There was a young man from Glengarrage
> The fruit of a scrofulous marriage
> Who sucked off his brother
> Then buggered his mother
> And ate up his sister's miscarriage.

More Dirty Jokes

More Dirty Jokes

More Dirty Jokes

More Dirty Jokes

More Dirty Jokes

More Dirty Jokes